PASSING CARS

The Internal Monologues of a Neurodivergent Trans Girl and Other Essays

MARISSA ALEXA MCCOOL   KAREN L. GARST

AMY LAVALLE HANSMAN

KIMBERLY ELEANOR PANNELL

AIDEN XAVIER MCCOOL

BETHANY L. FUTRELL   SARAH MAE EKHOLM

CHRISTOPHER REED   AMINA SHEPHERD

NATHAN DICKEY   DESSI CONNER

TONY OPELT   TIM BROWN   LOGAN REISS

Edited by
AMBER BIESECKER

Cover by
TERRY SHEFFIELD

CONTENTS

Books by Marissa   v

Acknowledgments   ix

Foreword   xi

Introduction   xv

STAGE I

Runaway   3

Domestic Abuse   11

Why Didn't You Just...?   17

STAGE II

Kicking Down the Door   23

Ambush   29

The Moment After   37

The Sick and Dying Have Plenty of Time to Think   39

Feminism Theater   45

From Shitlord to SJW   53

A Reflection on #MeToo   61

STAGE III

Managing the Fire   71

Crisis of Faith   75

Senses   79

Title Goes Here   81

STAGE IV

The Hard Truth   101

Let People Feel   103

Hang on Tighter   109

Loss   115

Coping With Loss   121

STAGE V

Name Day   127
Coming Out   133
My Love... The One I Married, Anyway   141
Coming Out Adult   147
What to Expect When You're Transitioning   149
Stage Fright   157
Many a Monologue   161

About the Author   177

BOOKS BY MARISSA

The PC Lie

False Start

Silent Dreams

Voice in the Dark

PODCASTS BY MARISSA

Inciting Incident

The Cis are Getting Out of Hand

Storytime with Rissy

Doubting Dogma

FTM: For Trans Men

We Too – Our Stories

To Aiden, Devyn, Michael, Kiernan, Nathaniel, and Logan.

And to Callie Wright, Ari Stillman, Molly Un-Mormon, and Bethany Futrell too.

ACKNOWLEDGMENTS

Lucinda Lugeons; Karen Garst; Chris Kluwe; Annie E. Clark and Andrea L. Pino; my parents, grandparents, and family (both blood and chosen); Thomas Smith; Eli Bosnick; Anna Bosnick; Noah Lugeons; Heath Enwright; Tom Curry; Cecil Cicirello; Amber Biesecker; Brian, Erin, and Alice Johns; Monica Speca; Molly Coddle Kimberly Pannell; Kelly LaRoe; Meta Mazaj; Maron Kant; Bridget Swanson; Rosemary Malague; Asa Jack Frederick; Kandi Emm; Brian Beccia; Kathryn Keiper-Smith; Ben Cleveland; Jess Ramaker; Raija Langhoff; Sarah Combellick-Bidney; Jenny Dix; Celes Dryer; Fish Townsend; Jorja Petersen; Pearl Lo; Chris Kapp; Terry Sheffield; Andreina Lamas; Alix Jules; Hemant Mehta; Kristi Winters; Jesse Dollermore; Brittany Page; Shelley Segal; Dan Arel; Zach Law; Lauren Martin Day; Cortney Murphy; Wendy Marsman; Stephanie Zvan; Jeremiah Traeger; James Hamblin; Trav Mamone; Jason Brocious; Brian Fields; Alisha Ann; Haley Renae; Melina and El Barratt; Sarah Hart; Sarah Tulien; Ashley Beisley; The Ladies Lounge; Kayla Hunt Currivan; Boneshaker Books; Christopher Reed, Kyle Steenblik, and Felicia Entwhistle; Dara Hoffman-Fox; Dean

Ohmsford; Michael Schaffer; The Cellar Door Skeptics; Bryce Blankenagel; Steve Shives; and Tim Brown.

And everyone who contributed or otherwise helped with this book, everyone I may have forgotten by accident, everyone who is a Patreon donor to one or more of my shows, and everyone who has ever written to me, come on my podcasts, had me on theirs, or otherwise supported me in my journey.

FOREWORD

KAREN L. GARST

It has been over a century since Marcel Proust wrote his seven-volume novel entitled *Remembrance of Things Past*. Spurred by the taste of a little cake called a madeleine, he delved into his past through the theme of involuntary memory.

This type of memory occurs when a cue in the present reminds us of something that has happened in the past. Scientists have discerned that emotional memories leave stronger traces in the brain. This is likely because the conscious memory is stored in one part of the brain and the emotional memory in another, thus giving these memories a double-whammy. Those that caused us pain or joy are the ones which come back to us the most often and are the most vivid.

Each of the essays in this collection is ripe with *remembrance of things past*. Marissa recalls the day she tried to leave home and heard the pounding of the basketball as it hit the rim and the asphalt as her father played.

It is not unusual for sounds and music to accompany a vivid memory. Colors can also be present, as when Aiden recalled that the sky was blue right before the accident, but that he remembered nothing about the accident itself.

These authors examine their memories to probe questions like, "When did I know I was transgender?" or "How did my father dying when I was a young child shape my life?"

Exploring the memories that occur in a serendipitous fashion such as in the Proust example, or via a more conscious probing of our past, helps us understand and anchor the person we are today.

But even more important is the courage shown by these authors who confront these memories head-on and push forward in spite of the pain and sorrow the memories have caused.

Many people never recover from the traumatic events they endured when they were children. These authors have, and should be acknowledged not only for the work they have done to deal with these experiences, but to share them so that others can benefit from what they have learned.

I feel compelled to share one of my own painful memories as well. When I was twenty-one, a boy asked me out in my hometown for a New Year's Eve party. He was a year older, and I didn't have much memory of him from high school.

After the event, he asked me what I thought about marrying a doctor. I was so inexperienced. Having been raised in a religious home, I knew very little about love, sex, or relationships. I was only taught that I must remain a virgin until I married.

He drove me back to college and we fooled around a bit. I didn't even know that my body could produce such amazing sensations. Imagine—twenty-one and I'd never masturbated!

He went off to his university and I spent the next six months in Paris. The memory of the day I received the Dear Jane letter is so clear. I was laying in my small bed on the seventh floor of a hotel in the Latin Quarter. I just knew there would be a letter in my mailbox that day. And there was. I sent his class ring back to him on the foot of a little troll I had purchased for him in Sweden.

This incident wouldn't have amounted to much if he hadn't called me back at the end of summer promising to "make it all up to me." This time we "went all the way," of course without the use of birth control. He went back to school, and even though we talked on the phone, I never saw him again.

Luckily, I didn't get pregnant, but I did call him when I was home at Christmas. I felt he owed me an explanation. He said he would call, but of course, he didn't.

When I reflect on this memory now, I give myself some credit for having had the courage at least to call him. But this incident, like so many of those revealed in this book, haunted me for the next two decades.

My cultural upbringing taught me that I was now a "fallen woman," so I slept with pretty much every man I encountered. Having no support for learning about what a good relationship looked like, I had many that were not. Often, a change in career was spurred on by a break-up.

It is truly amazing to me that I met my future husband when I was thirty-eight, and we have been happily married ever since. At least the story had a good ending.

But this modicum of courage I showed as a young woman is nothing compared to the courage shown by the authors in this book. I know that I would never have been able to confront the decisions that they have faced at such young ages. I am not even sure I would be able to do it today at the ripe age of sixty-seven. And it is this courage to speak out and help others in similar situations that should be applauded.

Many of authors talk about their struggle with their gender identity. One writes about having to hide their identity and deny who they were. Living with this denial while constantly being reminded they might suffer the punishment of hellfire is child abuse, pure and simple.

In my writings, I often state that religion is the last cultural barrier to gender equality. While this usually refers to equality between men and women based on the subjugation of women by religion, it applies equally well to LGBTQ issues. What arguments do you hear most often in criticism of LGBTQ persons? The Bible condemns it. The church condemns it. We must support people who want to live an authentic life, be true to who they are, and be accepted by others.

Marissa has stepped out into the public sphere to show the struggle that transgender people go through in order to help those who are thinking about coming out to their family or friends. She makes an excellent point that we must accept people at their word and not judge them. Whether someone says they are transgender or are the victim of sexual assault, believe them. Offer your support. Try to understand their point of view. Don't substitute your own.

The lessons learned from this book are many. I hope that you enjoy it as much as I did. When you are done reading it, give it to a local LGBTQ support group so that others can profit from its wisdom.

—Karen L. Garst

Author of *Women Beyond Belief: Discovering Life without Religion* and *Women v. Religion: The Case Against Faith and for Freedom* (Spring 2018).

INTRODUCTION
MARISSA ALEXA MCCOOL

It would be nice to go back to a time where I could remember things clearly.

That used to be a mark of who I was: I remembered everything. I played a game with the kids on the sixth grade baseball team where I'd pretend to be a robot because I could recall anything from teacher quotes to baseball statistics.

This was before I knew I was transgender. Actually, to be more accurate, it was before I knew there was a word "transgender." I can't help it; it's how most of you reading this probably know who I am. It's hard to evaluate my life outside of that context, and everyone from Dan Ellis to Tom and Cecil has asked when I knew I was trans.

Knew I was trans? Mid-20s.

Knew I was named Marissa? 18.

Knew I was *different?* Now there's a question.

I was seven and I tore a hole in my jeans for the first time. I cried because I thought I would get in trouble. Not exactly normal for someone perceived to be a little boy. My parents told that story many times, and would sigh in relief at the end because "he was a normal boy after all."

Sigh.

I was eight and I only wanted to hang out with girls. Most boys my age were into *Power Rangers*. I was into love stories. Baseball too, but I liked love stories, whether they were told in song or written form.

I was fifteen, and Susan was putting makeup on me. I loved the way I looked. Then I got that note from my girlfriend: "Please don't wear makeup tonight. It scares my friends."

I was eighteen, and pretending that it was drag. I was twenty-five and pretending it was cross-dressing. I was thirty and pretending that there weren't breasts growing under my Penn football jersey shirt.

I was out to the world, having published a book with Chris Kluwe and Eli Bosnick, but my parents didn't pick up on my hints. Somehow, they were the last to know.

That I was trans. That I had ADHD. That I had panic attacks. That I was autistic.

No matter how I tried to fight the image of being the rebellious, defiant eighteen-year-old punk. The one who dropped out of school, or more accurately, just never went. The one who bombed out of high school, or more accurately, was pushed out for not falling in line. The one who was still called "he," "sir," and "dude in a dress" long after my deadname was nothing but a memory.

So when did all this start?

I don't know. The concussions, autism, and PTSD have taken from me many different movies of memories. But I've always known I was different, and that should be enough of an explanation for why my oft-requested memoirs are written this way.

Because I'd never be able to write a full autobiography the way some would want me to. This is the next best thing:

Stories, my way, in the way I think, the way my brain processes, and the way I've always seen the world.

Only now I have the words I didn't have then.

The following events are true based on the best of my recollection through my neurodivergence and head injuries. Some of the names have been changed, others have not. Either way, I will only refer to those who are public figures by their full names.

Thank you for wanting to read the words that were, for so long, ramblings and incoherent waves of emotion in my head.

—Marissa Alexa McCool, June 9th, 2017
   12 hours after first consultation on gender-confirming surgery

STAGE I

Denial

"We all eat lies when our hearts are hungry."

—AUTHOR UNKNOWN

RUNAWAY

MARISSA ALEXA MCCOOL

Th   hese bags were way too heavy.
        I'd been carrying everything I could reasonably fit
into two giant trash bags. I was wandering through the
woods, hoping to avoid the authorities I knew were looking
for me. The last thing I'd heard was my dad bouncing the
basketball in the driveway.

Is this an isolated story from a much bigger overall
context? Definitely. Do I have the time to explain all of it?
Not really. Suffice it to say it was a bad day for everyone.

Back in the days when a cordless landline phone was a big
deal, I'd sometimes escape to my roof outside my bedroom
window. I really enjoyed being out in the sun and on the
phone at the same time, plus the roof gave me a sense of
peace and isolation that I often sought but seldom found. It
was hard enough keeping straight the emotions flying by me
at light speed; trying to address everyone else's concerns
made it even harder.

He was screaming at me once again. This wasn't a rare
occurrence. I was fifteen, a ninth-grader in the wrong body,
showing signs of neurodivergence and gender dysphoria that

were never spotted nor addressed, and going through the wrong puberty—it's no shock I was an emotional mess. I'm lucky things didn't end up worse.

I moved off the roof as soon as he told me to, but he kept yelling. Yelling at me for something I'd already stopped doing. Yelling at me for something that was, in my opinion, completely harmless. Yelling at me because, at that time, that's how it happened.

Once the yelling got to be too much—or as I would later call it in my life, my battery was too low—I snapped. I started yelling back at my mother and father. The words and obscenities weren't stopping like they usually did. Getting screamed at was nothing new, but this time it was pouring on. The accusations and insults were like butter falling from the knife of Danny Noonan at the ritzy gathering of rich fucks.

"I think I have enough butter now," my inner girl would say. It would come out as "Fuck you, I'm tired of this shit."

Raging testosterone was poison to me. So was the world expecting me to behave like an allistic person. It would be years before I would understand either.

Snapping was a lot harder to control when the words of hatred wouldn't end, or at least that's how my fifteen-year-old brain was taking them. How else was I supposed to feel? I didn't do things right. If I did them right, they weren't acknowledged. It was always about what I did wrong, or didn't do well enough, or forgot about.

The latter was the worst. I was always forgetting things, and I was always being accused of being lazy, unenthusiastic, or selfish. That made me more defiant. Not writing things down or keeping a calendar became an act of spite in a place where I felt like I had no power and my voice wasn't being heard.

Since the first day of sixth grade, my expectations vs. reality barometer from other people hadn't synced up. I heard about all the potential I had and how disappointed people were in me that I wasn't living up to it. They didn't know about the bullying. The slurs. The accusations. The hazing. The beatings. The harassment. Baseball bats were once involved. It got worse.

Then I was supposed to smile when I was playing baseball? All I was worried about was wanting to be safe. Actually, I was worried about wanting the *feeling* of safety. Even when I found it almost fifteen years later, it took a long time to process that it was okay that I wanted it, okay that I liked it, and okay that I wasn't living up to the preconceived notion that this is what a guy does. I'm not a guy. I'm not now. I wasn't then, either. I never have been.

But most people didn't know that, including me.

I said I was running away. They didn't believe me.

Even as I put all the belongings I could carry into a bag, they didn't believe me.

As I searched for anything I could reasonably carry on my back, they didn't believe me.

I opened the door, the sound barely registering against the pounding of the basketball on asphalt and rim, and still they didn't believe me.

But if I left, they were calling Detective Mason.

My friend Susan was rebellious too. She always talked about running away, being defiant against parental expectations, getting into trouble and not caring ... She wouldn't turn me in. Having no idea where she was, I did my best to find a payphone for hours. That determined my route.

By the time I'd reached the creek near our housing development, I knew both that people were going to find me if I was on the road, and that I had way too much shit in these bags. Plus, if I left them on the road or on the side of the trail, the cops or their dogs would pick up the scent. At least that's how the chase went in my mind.

I watched the first CDs I ever owned disappear under the brown water of the creek. I lightened the load to something reasonable for my scrawny fifteen-year-old arms to carry. I don't remember what I had or lost, but I know I lost things I could never get back. Memories sometimes come in non-specific flashes.

Once the trail led toward a road, I instead veered off into some unknowing soul's farmland. Seemed like the best way to get to the Pike. There was food on the Pike. There were payphones on the Pike. I needed to reach Susan before they found me.

I had no Google Maps, nor had I thought to grab a real one. I'd never paid attention how to get anywhere when my parents or friends would drive me places. My parents weren't going to let me drive soon anyway, so why bother? I certainly didn't have a cell phone of my own at that age.

My journey was based purely on a clueless series of guesses. My plan was staked solely on this idea that someone would take me in. The legal consequences of taking in a minor runaway had never entered my mind. Social cues and such things always took a long time to register with me. Some never did.

Walking along the Pike and hoping to find something to eat that wouldn't eat too far into the twenty-nine dollars and change I had somewhere in my bag, the four quarters in every payphone kept getting me the busy signal. Without realizing it at the time, I was actually walking much closer to my parents' house because I really didn't know the direction to Susan's. In retrospect, I wasn't even close to her place and would've been wandering a long time.

I wasn't thinking about that. Or anything else other than getting away from the yelling. The yelling was loud. The yelling was angry. I was tired of angry yelling.

I wanted to feel like I mattered, instead of being put back

in the behavioral health center where I'd once again be reminded that it was all my fault. My confusion: my fault. The yelling: my fault. The beatings: my fault. The bullying: my fault. The assault: my fault.

Circumstances and context were not taken into equation, only that I'd written some graphic hate poetry about my father, and that meant there was something wrong with me.

I was broken. I needed to be fixed. I needed to be supervised.

I was a failure. I wasn't living up to my potential. I didn't show any respect. I didn't live up to expectations.

I didn't like golf enough. I wasn't enthusiastic enough playing baseball.

I didn't like being screamed at. I didn't like being hit. I didn't like wanting to die.

I didn't like my penis.

I didn't like anything.

Except when my friends would take me away for weekends, and some parents would ask afterward if I ever got hugged. Or I'd be with Brenton, who kept me for entire weekends where we'd do nothing but write shit to girls on AOL and go to the Uni-Mart for Mountain Dew and Cheetos. Or his sister would hit on me, and I was clueless about how to handle it. I was clueless a lot.

Clueless and Oblivious: A Marissa McCool Story.

I reached Susan once it was dark. I was in the Hess gas station parking lot, and she said she'd call me back after asking where I was. She called back the number and kept me on the line until the police showed up.

She'd turned me in, being alerted to it, I'd find out later, by my parents logging onto my AOL account and sending messages to everyone on any of my mailing lists.

I'd never stood a chance.

In the back of the police car, I started kicking the door

like a maniac. There was a tick on my leg, and I was handcuffed. I couldn't get it off. I knew what those things could do. I finally got their attention, and someone took care of it for me.

Why was I being detained like a criminal? Had I broken the rules by wanting to be safe? Had I committed a crime because I didn't want beer breath laced with four-letter words sending me into what I'd later discover were panic attacks?

Was I troubled, or a criminal? My school and the behavioral center barely made any distinction to my satisfaction.

They drove me to the Carlisle Hospital instead of Holy Spirit. They put me in a room with a dome-shaped window heading inside. I wasn't even allowed to have shoelaces, because of course the sad kid was going to hang themselves.

Nobody understood me. They were much more interested in telling me what they knew about me, or how my thoughts and emotions lined up with this, or how I wasn't responsible, or how I was screwing up my life, or, as always, how I wasn't good enough.

I only wanted to not fear going to school and not fear coming home. I only wanted to not see another one of my friends commit suicide. I only wanted to not get beaten up again for being too feminine, too different, or for no fucking reason at all. Kids are awful.

They kept me in the dome room for four hours. I wasn't allowed to sleep. I had to ask to use the damn bathroom. It was solitary confinement.

Everywhere else ended up being full, so they sent me back to my behavioral health center like a repeat offender—that goddamn Catholic hospital where caffeine was bad and they'd tell my girlfriend's mother that I said I didn't ask to see her, thus ruining my relationship and any chance to see her.

I hated that place then and I hate it now. I wonder how

much electroshock they would've ordered if they'd found out I was both gay and a girl? Probably enough to make Mike Pence cream his slacks.

It was the only time in my life, to the day of this writing, that I'd ever ridden in the back of an ambulance. Fortunately for me, this time the Catholics putting me in a room and banning me from existing for a week totally worked out, and everything was fine from there on out for the rest of forever...

DOMESTIC ABUSE

DESSI CONNER

I n every situation imaginable, we come up with ways we would hypothetically deal with things.

For example, if we were about to become a victim of a car crash and the scene was set on a country road, no one else around for miles but you, and the other vehicle and the land next to you was smooth, flat land easily to pull in or out of, the two possibilities are:

A) Keep going or slow down and let the crash happen the way it should—which I am almost positive no one would allow if it was possible to avoid.

B) Swerve off the road and on to the land next to you, which would keep all safe and the least damage to your car. Win-win for everybody, right?

There are even more extreme thoughts that flow through our heads, what if's: a murder, a plane crash, would you kill-or-be-killed situations, or if your other half cheats, what would your reaction be?

Or what about something that happens every single day? To quote Kate Thornton, "We all like to think that if we were the victims of domestic abuse we'd up and leave," as did I. What happens when the day comes and you realize you are in a domestic abuse situation, which includes but is not limited to physical, emotional, mental, and spiritual abuse?

To quote Kate again, "... it's not always as easy or straightforward as that. Women stay with abusive partners for all kinds of reasons—they love them, they fear them, they have children with them, they believe they can change them, or they simply have nowhere else to go."

As for myself, I am a survivor of domestic violence. I have been beaten, choked, slapped, and put into the hospital. The worst part of it all? The emotional damage.

Physical wounds heal while the emotional damage stays with you and becomes your own personal hell every single time you close your eyes. It literally changes everything about your life. Where you once was an overachiever, you are now a homebody, wrapped inside your blanket and bawling your eyes out because you cannot get the words or memories out of your mind.

You feel chained to your abuser still. As sick as it sounds, I'm sure they know that, and they get off on the fact that they above everyone else was the person who broke you. You can't get them off your mind. You don't understand why it had to happen.

Or when you start crying in public because you swore you saw someone who looked just like your abuser. No one understands. You are completely alone in your hellish prison.

This is only the aftereffect, after you leave the abuser. What about during? Most people say if it's that bad, then just leave. It isn't simple. It takes time, and planning, and the desire to want to leave. Once abuse starts and your own will gets broken down, the abuser implants their own intentions, desires, and needs into your mind. You aren't sure what is real, what are your thoughts, what are your feelings; what makes you you starts to slip away out of your hands.

Worry becomes your constant companion. Even down to the color of your socks, and no, I'm not joking.

I tried so hard to keep him happy, I would try my best to cook better, clean better, sleep with him better, not argue back any longer, keep my head down, and wait on him hand and foot. Even then, that wasn't enough. Keeping a journal of what was said by him word for word and hiding it to make sure I was, in fact, not going crazy.

Your memories are real, because they will challenge that. They might talk you into quitting your job to stay home, and then when money gets tight, they might yell and blame you. "Well, if you didn't quit your job, we wouldn't be in this mess. It is all your fault!"

How about when you come to them calmly and try to explain your feelings to them? Then they can and will twist whatever comes out of your mouth invalidate your feelings, and make you seem like a horrible person for even thinking or feeling the way that you do. They'll suggest you stop seeing your family, your friends, and if you do, prepare for all hell to break loose when you get home.

Every twist and turn in life will somehow be your fault. Even if you couldn't have possibly had any control of the situation—like them getting fired from their job or their tire going flat on the highway.

Now, I know you are still asking the question, "If it was so bad, why did you stay?"

One of the many key parts of being an abuser is making your victim feel confused. Confused about their love for you. They will make you hate them, they will make you love them, they will make you feel as if your happiness can only be given through them. They will turn anything and anyone against you.

My ex loved to keep me high on weed. If I was high after a big fight, he knew I would forget and forgive way too easily. He would wrap me in his arms and whisper sweet nothings to me, empty promises accompanied with tears as he swore he would change and reminded how much he loved me.

He would stare into my eyes, and in those sweet, soft moments I could feel our souls crashing into each other like waves. My eyes would drip tears, my soul would bust open from the love he poured into it, my arms would reach for him, and my mind would be too foggy with the drug to fight the compulsion of his words.

After I left, I was confused. I knew I did the right thing, but why did I feel like I needed him so badly? Why did I call and text and ask him to come stay the night with me? I was so lost.

For two and a half years I was told how to think and feel. I didn't understand what my own will and desires were any longer. I needed confirmation that I was good enough, that I was beautiful enough. I needed to be told where I belonged in the world.

He'd stripped everything and everybody away from me. I didn't have a friend or family member left. I didn't have a job, and I sure as hell didn't own anything any longer. My car and belongings was taken from me during the relationship, sold to the highest bidder. When he left, he even left me with a stack of unpaid bills.

I was lost. I became a drunk. I wasn't able to control myself. How does one control themselves after they haven't had control over their own life for over two years?

It's been two years since, and two years ago I thought of myself as a victim, but now I label myself as a survivor. I survived hell—my personal hell. I broke the chains I allowed to be placed on my very own mind.

I became my very own person, and I will tell you, it wasn't

easy. Restarting my life from the beginning and trying to heal myself mentally was the hardest thing I've ever had to overcome. Physical abuse doesn't even start to add up to the amount of damage mental abuse had caused in my life.

My name is Dessi, and I am a survivor.

WHY DIDN'T YOU JUST...?

MARISSA ALEXA MCCOOL

I was sexually assaulted in the summer of 2014.

Since that time, I have read countless stories, talked to countless people, and seen countless events unfold where people have been assaulted, threatened, abused, and worse. There's one thing that they all seem to have in common, more or less: Someone saying "Why didn't you just X?"

Maybe X is "Why didn't you just leave if he was abusing you?" or "Why didn't you just call the police if you were assaulted?" Regardless of what X is, it's indicative of a first reaction that a good percentage of people seem to have when listening to someone else's story—the instinct to find out what they could've done differently, or what they did wrong, or what they didn't do in time, or how they didn't handle it.

"Why didn't you just X?" is the epitome of victim-blaming, at least as much as "we live in such a victim culture" is a kiss-off to those who have suffered assault or abuse.

The shift of blame making it to the person who violated consent or harmed another person is hard to traverse. Whether it's the school not knowing what to do or a friend not knowing how to help, their actions are almost secondary in the eyes of many. "It couldn't have been that bad if you stayed" or "maybe you said yes, but just regretted it afterward."

I don't think it's a lack of empathy. I think it's symptomatic of a system that has been put in place to not deal with people getting away with shit. It protects those who are just being young or throwing a ball or not wanting their lives to be ruined forever by removing the consent from another person and taking something that isn't theirs. Why these systems are in place, I'm not sure, but they're there.

Any post you encounter on Facebook of someone talking about these things will not only be met with these victim-blaming questions, but will also have comparative questions of their agency. "They don't live in the Middle East, so it can't be that bad." "They survived, so it can't be that bad." There's always an excuse for why it happened. There's always an excuse for why it could've been worse.

Meanwhile, a person is having a panic attack when they see their attacker every single day, and the campus police are too busy asking what they wore. There's bureaucratic nightmares lying between the victim and justice of any kind. There are untested rape kits, hidden stories, avoiding of bad PR, and Gaslighting Central from abusers who either don't know they're abusers or want to keep getting away with it.

So many people want to blame the person who was assaulted. So many people want to blame the person who was abused.

I don't know what to do about this. No matter how many speak out about their stories, there are shitty people looking to make it the fault of the person who received this treatment, rather than confront a culture that protects and welcomes these behaviors, or at least excuses them with anything from "that's how it happens in romantic movies" to "boys just being boys."

I didn't go to the cops when I was raped for multiple reasons. I'm a trans person, so they'd likely think it was my fault for existing, that me being open and public was an invitation to such behavior, since some people link us being trans with some kind of sexual fetish or perversion. A woman did it, and enough people think that in and of itself is impossible. And because I spent so much time, even to this day, asking the very questions that so many people throw on the abused and the victimized, still blaming myself on some level.

When people get abused or raped, because of how this society treats those who have been, it's nearly impossible to not internalize these victim-blaming tendencies. "I could've done better." "I should've seen it coming." "I should've gotten out earlier." "I should've trusted my instincts."

Because so many people are set against believing us or finding any way that it couldn't have possibly been the perpetrator's fault, at least entirely, we start to believe it ourselves.

When I was the recipient of repeated unwanted touching earlier this year, my first self-criticism wasn't on how better to protect myself, but on how I didn't say "no" assertively enough. On how I put myself in a position for that to happen. On how I should've known better.

In other words, victim-blaming is so common that I ended up doing it to myself.

If that isn't indicative that we have a major problem when it comes to helping those who have suffered these situations, I don't know what is. But I can tell you this: if someone comes to you and tells you that they've been abused, attacked, assaulted, or anything else ...

Instead of asking what they were doing or how they could've stopped it or suggesting what they could've done differently, start by telling them that you believe them. Just knowing that someone in the world to whom they've trusted enough to admit these events believes you is a step that many people need in order to start coping with what happened in the first place.

One that happens all too seldom in the stories of many. I've even seen recently when women quote statistics of how many people are assaulted or have been abused, someone will inevitably respond, "That seems a bit high."

Yeah. It is. And the fact that your first reaction is disbelief does nothing but prove that further. Stop blaming people for what abusers, assaulters, rapists, and violators have done and start supporting those they've hurt rather than trying to find out what they could've done better to stop it in your eyes. If you've ever wondered why more people don't speak up or step forward, your answer lies in those reactions.

Believe people when they tell you something's happened to them. Start there, and then move forward with the rest.

STAGE II

Anger

"The real violence, the violence I realized was unforgivable, is the violence we do to ourselves when we're too afraid to be who we really are."

—NOMI MARKS, *SENSE8*

KICKING DOWN THE DOOR

MARISSA ALEXA MCCOOL

Six days after the election had most of the Penn campus in absolute fear. What was going to happen to us? Were we safe? How were we going to get through four years of this?

Within days of the election, someone had invited all the black freshmen to a lynching group, Nazi symbols were appearing everywhere, and the problem was those of us affected by this because we needed our safe spaces and therapy dogs. Of course; the true problem was just that the world was too safe for anyone who wasn't a cis-het white man, so naturally we needed to take care of that shit because sometimes college students yelled.

I was sitting in Creative Non-Fiction writing with one of the best professors I ever had, Dr. Marion Kant. She and I seemed to be the only ones in the class with a true grasp of how scary the situation really was.

Having only just started presenting, as Pastor Carl was less than a month prior, I was terrified that I'd have to go back into the closet; not just to be safe, but to survive. I knew that we were the targets of the MAGA bullshit, and then from the other side of the "everyone is too PC and SJWs ruin everything for caring about other people," or whatever version of that was running at the time.

The first half of the three hour class was nothing more than us trying to make sense of what the world was going to be. There was only one guy in the class, and we were all terrified on some level. Without even really thinking about it, the space that was open for my notes on the class began filling with words.

That weekend, I'd spent in Fort Lauderdale with a few close friends. The road trip through the deep south was even more terrifying than usual, as those on the winning side of the election seemed more emboldened than ever. It's still a reality that we have to be absolutely terrified of when or where we can use the bathroom. Or, as some people call it, limited government out of your lives.

I type 100 words a minute as it is, but I was destroying my keyboard in that class; all the while participating in the discussion. I'd spent nearly four hours ranting into a microphone on the way back from Florida, and I was in no mood for compromise, apologetics, or trying to reason how bad it might not be. As a recently out trans person, I not only had a pretty good feeling about how bad it could be and would get, but I also knew that anything that involved protecting us that the Obama administration had set forth would be in serious danger almost immediately.

Glancing down after a long while, I realized I had thirty pages. Apparently I had a lot to say. It was at that moment that I not only decided to make it a book, but the days of being passive and avoiding confrontation were over. That mentality had gotten us a more dangerous world for bullies, racists, homophobes, transphobes, and those who would excuse their actions in the name of free speech. Allies were going to be few, and I didn't have time for them to explain their supposed rationality.

Having just interviewed Chris Kluwe on election night, he was the first person I emailed. First, I came out to him, as I wasn't out on Inciting Incident yet, and then I asked him to write the foreword for the book I was going to make. I wanted to get it out before the inauguration and include as many voices as possible. He agreed right away, and like many people who aren't terrible, changed the name he called me and the pronouns he used instantaneously. Gee, it's almost like it's not that hard or something.

The rest of the 17 chapters, I wrote within the next nine days, all the while summoning support from other writers who were rightfully terrified for the well-being of those they loved. I wasn't too interested in the apologetics that reasoned that it wasn't going to be as bad as we thought, or that they didn't vote for Trump because of his bigotry. That didn't matter. Whether they voted for him for that reason or not, they still excused it. If it wasn't the reason, it wasn't enough to persuade them out of someone who advocated for sexual assault, among the many other horrific things he said, all in the name of what was or wasn't "politically correct."

That was when I had it; I needed a title that truly spelled out how I felt about the entire ridiculous "PC" argument. Every time I heard someone complaining about it, it seemed to be in response to not being allowed to call somebody a slur or insult them in some way. That was the only time free speech mattered; in regard to being an asshole. Therefore, a title that encompassed bluntly how I felt about it would be it. The subtitle was as subtle as a trainwreck: How American Voters Decided I Don't Matter. In retrospect, I should've made it "We Don't Matter," as there are a great number of groups affected by his inane policies and pitiful attempt at leadership.

Puerto Ricans, for example, who were finally important enough to receive jump shots with paper towels after dealing with devastating hurricanes. But that was really their fault because they had Hispanic-sounding last names, right? What a joke.

Names that I had only admired were suddenly paying attention to me, within the skeptic podcasting community and beyond. This wasn't my first journey into creating. At that point, I'd had almost 70 episodes of Inciting Incident. I'd written five books; four of which nobody really paid any attention to, and I'd done a YouTube show for four years with dreams of making it to Channel Awesome.

Now, not only were people listening to what I was saying, they were pre-ordering my book. People who I never thought would care about anything I made now wanted signed copies. It was completely new to me, or at least completely new to what I allowed myself to take in from others.

The main thing was, anything I'd created before that point, I wasn't truly in. The deadname that I used, that most people knew me by, was not at all who I was. It was a mirage, a front; something I still maintained out of fear for what might happen. That was no longer an option.

The previous time of trying to come out and facing what I did left me in a numbness that took years to get over. The void that I felt from knowing who I truly was but hiding from it was the worst thing I'd ever known, and I was no longer willing to concede that for the comfort of people who didn't understand or who weren't willing to accept it. Their adjustments were no longer my problem.

I was and forever had been Marissa, a girl, who I truly was inside. I'd gone from "use whatever pronouns I'm presenting" to male pronouns feeling like a stab in the heart. I wasn't in my own work. Rewatching old episodes of my YouTube show, I felt like I wasn't saying anything, or at least anything that mattered. My podcast was somewhat better, but even then, when making references to LGBT rights, especially trans issues, I referred to how I was feeling in the third person, as if that would be consolation enough.

Callie Wright had used the tag line at the end of her show to tell me directly that an entire community was waiting to embrace me. Yes, she always said it at the end of *The Gaytheist Manifesto*, but that night I'd interviewed her, I'd come out to her prior to the interview, much the same way as I would to Eli Bosnick several months later, and I read the subtext. Now he'd be contributing an essay to my book. How things had changed since everything in the world changed on a dime.

Within a few months, I'd gone from being in the closet to kicking down the closet door with a book that began with the words "fuck you," the same ones I'd ended my rant at Pastor Carl with, and I'd changed my preferred name with the University. Where before I'd rushed too quickly, this time I hit the ground running with no regret whatsoever.

While I hate that it was this election that made me break those barriers and become authentic, it might not have happened otherwise. Sometimes there's an, if you'll pardon the pun, inciting incident that alters the projected timeline of your life. I don't know where mine was going before all this transpired, but I definitely chose the better path, everything considered. You're reading this, aren't you?

AMBUSH

AMY LAVALLE HANSMAN

I realized I was walking into an ambush as soon as I entered the room. I had been led to believe it was going to be another routine meeting between myself and the school counselor. My eleven-year-old son had already missed nearly forty days of the sixth grade due to his anxiety disorder, and it was only November.

But let me back up a little. My son had been diagnosed with generalized anxiety disorder and "OCD tendencies" when he was ten. We had spent a solid year taking him to therapy every week, only to see zero improvement in his near daily panic attacks. So we finally took the leap and put him on Zoloft.

He'd had some wonderful teachers in the fifth grade that took him under their wings and got him through the year in one piece. I'll be forever grateful to those teachers for their ability to go above and beyond for my child. But now it was sixth grade, and shit was getting serious.

Sixth grade is important. It will make or break the entire rest of your life. It's that time when a kid needs to really buckle down and think about what they're going to do with their life.

This is what brought me to this room on this day in November. My son had just started taking Zoloft, and I was cautiously optimistic about the direction things were going. I was eager to talk to School Counselor about the small, but encouraging improvement I had seen in my son, and discuss where to go from here to keep him caught up with his schoolwork.

But when I looked around the table in the small conference room, I saw more than just School Counselor. I also saw School Counselor #2, Dean of Students, Vice Principal, Math Teacher, Science Teacher, and School Nurse.

School Nurse and I were old friends. She had been on a crusade to keep the school's archaic abstinence-only sex-ed curriculum in place, and I had been on a mission to change it. We had sparred openly at a school board meeting just one month before. So yeah, her presence at that table really put me at ease.

School Counselor began by thanking me for coming and asking why my husband couldn't make it to the meeting. I told them he couldn't get out of work, which was the truth. Had I known this meeting was going to be an ambush, I would have made better arrangements to have him by my side.

But I didn't know. So I was here alone.

School Counselor said that all of these people who had come to the table on this day were very concerned about my son's attendance issues. I was concerned about my son's attendance issues too. I thought to myself, "Fuck, my *whole life* at the moment is my son's attendance issues."

I frantically explained to the group of authority figures in the room all of the things we were doing to try and get my son's anxiety under control. I tried to get them to understand that this wasn't anything we were taking lightly. We had put our kid on medication, for Christ's sake! We had dealt with the judgement from friends, family, and random strangers about putting our eleven-year-old on an antidepressant. I tried to get them to understand. I tried to get them on *my side*.

But they weren't on my side. Not really. To them, my child had become a problem. A hassle. A pain in the ass. Just another one of the many hundreds of kids in a sea of kids that they had to *deal with* on a daily basis. He had long since maxed out the number of "sick days" he was allowed to have, and now they had to get him "back on track." Get him humming along like the other hundreds of kids in the sea of students who just had to suck it up and get to school every day.

Math Teacher piped up to let me know that my son was a great kid who did well when he was at school. I had heard this from basically every teacher my son had ever had. He was a great kid. Smart. Kind. Hardworking. Not a troublemaker. A joy to be around. So they simply couldn't understand what the problem was.

Math Teacher was "old school," a thirty-year veteran teacher who was getting too old for this shit. And while he didn't say it out loud, I could practically hear the monologue happening in his head. The same monologue I imagine has gone through the minds of many teachers:

"These kids and their 'diagnoses.' <insert dramatic eye roll here> Honestly, every kid seems to have a 'diagnosis' these days, when we all know the real problem is just having parents who coddle them and let them get away with endless nonsense and have failed to instill a solid work ethic in them. Basically, they've all become 'soft.' Sure, school isn't always fun. Get over it. Life isn't always fun. Suck it up. Deal with it."

I told Math Teacher, and the rest of the room, that what they didn't see was the kid I had to deal with every day.

The kid who couldn't get to sleep on school nights and sent me text messages from his bedroom until midnight or later telling me he just couldn't get to sleep.

The kid who, every morning before school, would wake himself up at 5:00 a.m. just so he'd have a full two hours to decompress before he had to face the day.

The kid who, on more mornings than not, would start shaking and crying and dry-heaving as the time to leave for school approached.

The kid who would hold his aching stomach and sob, doubled over, begging me not to make him go to school.

I told everyone at the table about the heartbreak my son and I went through every morning, all because his brain simply couldn't handle the thought of being in a building all day where he had no control.

Where he couldn't retreat to his bedroom when the anxiety got the better of him. Where he had to deal with the fear of failure every day. Where he had to face lunchrooms full of noisy pre-teens and classrooms full of kids who just couldn't follow the rules, and why can't they just follow the rules, and don't they clearly know the rules?!

And to make matters worse, there was nothing specific in the school we could point to and "fix" to make things better for him. There was no obvious bully. He had good friends. He liked most of his classes.

But none of that mattered. It was all about his own lack of control to manage his day. About being in the right place at the right time, and not standing out too much. About using all of his mental energy to "fake it" and not show his issues to anyone else.

Then School Nurse spoke up to ask me what my son does all day when I let him stay home because of these alleged "stomach aches" (the stomach aches which plague him, and aren't a symptom of a medical illness, but a physical manifestation of his mental illness).

What I thought was, "Fuck you, lady. It's none of your goddamned business what he does when he's at home, you fundamentalist Christian monster."

What I said was that he usually stays in bed and watches TV. I don't let him play video games or do anything on his computer. But I don't have the heart to make him stare at the wall all day. And I have a job. I don't have time to do enriching activities with him when he's not at school.

To which School Nurse helpfully replied, "Well, if he's just sitting around at home with a stomach ache, is there some reason he can't sit in school with a stomach ache?"

And what I thought was, "You really are a heartless fucking monster, aren't you? Do you enjoy going to work with a relentless stomach ache?!"

And what I said was... nothing, because I was looking at her, stunned.

School Nurse went on to let me know that my son could always just ask to go to the nurse's office when he was having his alleged "stomach aches" to take a break and regroup for class. I told her that he'd tried that, many times. But what he'd learned was that the nurse on duty would wait for him to literally vomit right in front of her before calling his mom to pick him up.

And that was his end goal—to get someone to come and pick him up and take him away from this place.

If he didn't have a temperature, and if he wasn't vomiting in front of them, it was straight back to class with his malingering nonsense. So he'd learned that the nurse's office had nothing to offer him.

I told School Nurse that my kid wasn't stupid and that he had access to Google. I wondered out loud how long it would take him to figure out how to make himself vomit on demand.

School Counselor had now grown tired of this conversation, and dramatically flipped a sheet of paper back and forth in front of him, presumably looking at the long list of absences my son had racked up to date. With a red face, he told me that this number of absences was *unacceptable*, and he wanted to know what I was going to do to *fix it*. He told me that what my kid really needed was some "tough love." After all, he did just fine wearing a mask in front of his teachers at school, so the problem must be at home.

It was then that I started to cry. And I was immediately angry with myself. Because not only was I crying in front of that mega-bitch, School Nurse, but I was proving to everyone at the table that I was the weak, pushover mother they had assumed me to be. I'd proven that this really *was* my fault.

With those tears, I'd confirmed that I couldn't handle stress. That I buckled under pressure. That I'd let my kid push my buttons and con me into staying home from school.

And I felt that blame, deeply. I thought to myself, "Oh my god, they're right! This *is* all my fault! What if I've fucked up parenting so badly that I've ruined my child? I *knew* I shouldn't be trusted with a kid! I knew it from the moment I walked out of the hospital with him after he was born, and no one stopped me or made me take a class or read a manual or promise to check in with someone responsible on a daily basis to make sure I wasn't colossally fucking everything up!"

I told the assembly of grim faces around the table that the only thing I could think to do was to lock myself in a room every morning where my son couldn't reach me and break my heart and beg me to stay home. I told them I'd just have to let his dad deal with him, because his dad could leverage his deep "dad voice" to get our son to comply with the demands to go to school. He could leverage our son's fear of making his dad angry to get him to school every day (or at least, most of the days).

And it was going to be hard for me (for all of us, really), but I was willing to do it if it meant reversing all of the damage I'd singlehandedly done to my child. I was willing to sacrifice my son's relationship with his dad to get him into this building every day.

And the assembly of smug faces accepted that answer. They thought it sounded reasonable. School Nurse handed me a tissue and told me that it was very important for a boy to have a strong male role model in the home (something she undoubtedly read in some shitty James Dobson book), and the rest of the table concurred and nodded approvingly.

This was a good plan. This would work.

And I left, still crying as I walked to my car. And I felt like shit. I felt like the worst parent who'd ever tried and failed to raise a child properly.

And later that night, I'd tell my son that the school was simply not going to let him stay home anymore. And I'd hold him while he has the worst panic attack he'd ever had. And he'd beg me to take him to the hospital because he couldn't breathe and his heart was beating too fast and he was sure he might be dying.

And I wouldn't take him to the hospital. Instead, I'd hold him and watch YouTube videos of doctors explaining how to get through a panic attack, and I'd breathe with him. I'd give him some of the PRN medication the psychiatrist gave me for really bad situations. I'd watch a DVD of the Puppy Bowl with him while he rocked back and forth and cried, until he finally, mercifully, drifted off to sleep.

THE MOMENT AFTER

MARISSA ALEXA MCCOOL

T he scent of damp bodily function wafted through the pitch-dark room. Slow, heavy breaths scored the otherwise oppressive silence. The clenching fingers were at war with the downy threads raging against each other, a single beat of sweat dripped down a glistening, furrowed brow. Breathing, unlike other instantly previous actions, was minimally consensual.

Nervous metatarsals gripped the cold, wooden panels forming the pathway of momentary escape. The racing thoughts converged with the methodical, deliberate pace with which reprieve is gained. Solace found only in the hidden comfort of solitude; presence regained its autonomy after its ultimate but temporary betrayal.

Being alone is figurative, as the violator remains immediately above the present state of the stripped. The past force exerted to gain physical superiority continues to press firmly into the crushed veins and nerves of exacerbated vulnerability. Muse's cruel inspiration drips through the ethereal blackness, much like the foreign wetness invading the chambers of once-held peace. In silence, there cannot be a calm that washes away these drops of unforgivable malice.

Eyes eventually close, parting bittersweetly with the shock-induced numbness before trauma truly sets in the system. A subconscious reprieve is the only savior from the uncaring hand of reality reinstating its monarchy over the peasants of cope. But, like all monarchs, long shall they live, cruel shall they reign.

But not tonight.

THE SICK AND DYING HAVE
PLENTY OF TIME TO THINK
BETHANY L. FUTRELL

I t was 2011, and I was dying. I knew something was terribly, horribly wrong, and I knew it was my kidney that was giving me so much pain. A couple of years before, I had passed my very first kidney stone, and it hurt like you wouldn't believe. That first experience, however, gave me a strong, vivid memory of what it feels like to have your kidney blow up like a balloon and try to kill you.

My doctor (or shall we say, the woman who had the title of "nurse practitioner") disagreed. She told me it was diverticulitis (nope), and that to be cured, I should stop eating nuts or anything spicy (my favorite, though!) and drink a glass of freshly squeezed lemonade every day.

Okay... sure. I can do that. I was a vegetarian at the time, so nuts were kind of important to my diet, but I could work around it. I really, really hate bland food, but doctor says! I was happy to try if the doctor said it was best. Doctors went to school for this, you know, and I didn't.

I realize now that I just wasn't physically well enough to think critically at the time. I didn't realize two simple things:

that sometimes doctors are wrong, and I was *not* seeing an actual doctor.

I still requested that they run some tests or scans to determine the problem because I recognized my pain, and it was in my kidney; I knew it. They declined.

Not long thereafter, disgusted with the bland food and getting seriously tired of lemonade, I was feeling worse and went back to the doctor's office, this time demanding that they run some tests. Although I was an adult, it took my mother going to bat for me before they would do anything. They scheduled a scan and ran an analysis begrudgingly.

When I arrived, alone, at another doctor's office for the ultrasound of my kidney, I didn't expect anything was really killing me. I had lost all that weight through my clean and healthy vegetarian diet, I thought. I had been a little woozy because I was reeling from getting away from an abusive partner, I thought. I was in pain because that yoga position had knocked loose a kidney stone, I thought.

I never once considered I might be dying, but the woman who was scanning my belly looked at me that day like no one else has ever looked at me. There was concern in her eyes, but also something else. Fear? Confusion? Astonishment? I found out later that what was going on inside me should have had me bedridden with pain.

They wouldn't let me leave. The various personnel in that office explained to me that there was a problem and that I needed more powerful scans immediately. My sister was at school. My mother was at the hospital across town with my stepdad (he's fine). I didn't have anyone with me, and I was terrified.

I went ahead and got the scan they suggested, and we waited for the doctor on site to look over the results. When they finally told me, I don't think I really heard all the words, just "immediately hospitalized." They didn't want me to drive, so one of the nurses walked me over to the hospital nearby and stayed with me through intake until my mother arrived.

When the surgeon came in, he did a double-take. I think I looked too healthy to be a dying girl; I had walked there on my own two feet, after all. He explained that the kidney had to come out, and soon.

Xanthogranulomatous pyelonephritis is extremely rare, but those two long words meant one little thing: my kidney was trying to kill me. I had learned my lesson from that "nurse practitioner," though, and instead of scheduling surgery then and there, my family drove me to yet another facility in another state to get a second opinion. That was a painful drive. The surgeon there agreed with the surgeon in my hometown, and we ended up scheduling the surgery on our way back home.

You may have had surgery, or maybe you haven't. If not, I can tell you that it is absolutely *no fun*. You're stuck in a hospital room for ages, and you're in pain, and the nurses come in every day in the wee hours of the morning to take your blood. There is nothing to do but watch TV and read and sit and wait.

And think.

Although I would never go back there on purpose, I do find myself surprisingly glad for that time in the hospital and the long recovery afterward. While I was waiting for my body to become whole again, I took the time to challenge my brain. I had grown up hyper-religious, but I had been questioning my faith.

So, with nothing better to do, I watched *all* the debates. I saw the greats on stage standing up for reason. Christopher Hitchens spoke so forcefully. Matt Dillahunty was a master at pointing out logical flaws and fallacies. All the while, the thing I noticed with a growing sense of disgust was that the arguments my fellow Christians were using were always the same.

Much like the woman who heard my complaints of pain and assumed she knew the answer already, the religious debaters consistently presented arguments for which there was no evidence and which had been previously refuted, and none of them seemed to notice. They reminded me of her when they wouldn't listen to the atheists' arguments. These were the Christians who were standing up for my god?

I pulled out all my apologetics reference books, and there were tons of them. I opened my Bible and began to search. I researched via apologetics websites. I looked through everything I had available to see if I could find any argument that wasn't the same old thing that I had heard in those debates over and over.

I wanted to be able to prove my god to myself (1 Peter 3:15). I couldn't. From what I could see, no one had.

But this isn't a story about how I became an atheist, although this is definitely when I threw off the shackles of faith. This story is about skepticism.

Prior to my illness, I was somewhat skeptical, but not in all areas and not enough. I should have been skeptical of my own thoughts about what was wrong with my body. I should have sought a second opinion the first time around. I should have asked questions when I was told I needed to be hospitalized. I should have seen the flaws in my perspective on god.

Even though I was right that my kidney was the problem, I never should have been so certain. Even though the doctors who hospitalized me were correct to do so, I should have questioned them. And even though it was painful and fruitless, it was right to seek a second opinion before letting someone cut out my organ.

That's the beauty of skepticism—the ability to see the

limits of one's own knowledge and the desire to seek more data everywhere. When you consistently question everything, you end up searching for more and more information in all areas of life.

That is what this story is about. Seeking knowledge.

During my recovery, which was unfortunately long and painful, I spent a great deal of my time seeking knowledge. I found support groups online and realized that the man I was dating before had truly been abusive, and I wasn't just imagining it. I discovered a wealth of information on religions around the world, and I learned to think more critically about their claims. I learned that one should not believe things without evidence.

But what really stuck with me was how to question and how to search for more information. Frankly, atheism was a side-effect of skepticism.

I should not have been in my twenties before I learned how to ask good questions and started putting that skill into practice. Skepticism is not some natural characteristic of our species; it is a skill that can be learned. Shouldn't we be teaching each other how to question? Shouldn't we be sharing that skill with our children? At the very least, shouldn't you question at least one thing you hear every day?

FEMINISM THEATER

MARISSA ALEXA MCCOOL

"Feminism is over," I often heard on UPenn's campus. "There's no need for it anymore. Look at how many women are here."

I didn't see any of those people when the hate preachers showed up with signs that said: "Women, get back in the kitchen."

"Men are really the ones discriminated against," I often heard in atheist groups. "We've won the fight against inequality, but now they want superiority over men."

I didn't see any of those people speaking up when the older, cisgender, straight white men decided that the responsibility for Trump lay at the feet of us trans people for the crime of wanting the right to use the bathroom, or when we were getting attacked for having the nerve to exist and stand up for ourselves.

"We support equality on all fronts," I'd often hear administration and staff say on campus. "We protect our students of all ethnic backgrounds, sexual orientations, and gender expressions."

I didn't see any of those people standing up to the hate

preachers. Instead, they were making sure that we didn't interfere with their right to free speech.

And by free speech, of course, they mean following young students around, shouting slurs, and harassing them in the public square.

But our right to tell them to go fuck themselves? That required security to escort us away. We wouldn't want to interfere with First Amendment rights, would we?

In the last few years, between my education at the University of Pennsylvania and becoming a somewhat-successful podcaster and author, I've heard a lot of rhetoric on many different sides of the feminism and activism spectrum. As a trans, queer, neurodivergent woman, one of the main problems I've identified is that words of support are often empty, tokenizing, and void of any meaning in the face of actually living up to them.

It's hard to believe there is an atheist movement at all, at least in the singular sense. On one hand, some of the best friends I've made since coming out are fellow atheist podcasters, fans, and friends, who have gone to bat for me every step of the way and been among the kindest, most supportive people I've ever met.

Yet in this supposedly unified movement, anyone who cares about feminism, racism, equality, LGBT rights, etc., is called a "social justice warrior," a "cuck," or shouted down for the crime of doing something like defining the word "intersectionality."

Wanting to exist in a space devoid of religious influence as someone who isn't a white man has brought me into a theater of discussion that is indistinguishable from the same conversations being held in religious circles, except the central visible force isn't necessarily the omnipotent being in the sky who says these rules must be so.

At those times, there are an awful lot of people who want

to play the centrism role and say that both sides are just as bad, and that feminists, SJWs, and whichever other pejorative they've come up with that's supposed to be a scathing criticism of our empathy—all of *them* are the real bullies.

With their safe spaces and censoring of free speech, they're as bad as Nazis, aren't they? I mean, one time, they shouted at someone on campus. That's clearly the same thing as spreading flyers around Cleveland State University encouraging LGBT youth to commit suicide, right?

I didn't spend the majority of my academic career as an out trans person. It took several years for me to discover the resources that were available to me. It wasn't until the suicide epidemic reached the double digits within a few years that the resources of CAPS and the LGBT Center were even mentioned in the mass emails.

However, when some of us desperately needed the administration on our side—or at least available resources in order to function as students in an increasingly difficult situation—the people to whom we were sent weren't really aware of what was needed.

There was one doctor at student health who could be seen about trans issues and questions. One. At a campus with 42,000 students.

Interspersed with that kind of "in spirit only" student life protection were students who spouted a lot of the buzzwords and beliefs, but always had a "but." By that I mean, "I support women's rights, but..." "I support LGBT rights, but..." "I believe in equality, but..."

However, they were sure to call themselves feminists, and were sure to let you know that they called themselves feminists. Only when it came time to stand up for someone or do something about it, they were noticeably absent.

Feminism Theater, as it were, was as present as feminist ideology and rhetoric.

I came out as transgender by screaming in the face of a hate preacher who had been on campus repeatedly during the weeks leading up to the 2016 election. Many on campus at the time were espousing the age-old belief that if you ignored bullies, they'd get bored and leave. Standing up to them was giving them the attention they wanted, and therefore enabling them to win, as if there was a scorecard and someone was tallying the victories and losses.

But when I saw this hate preacher walking around Locust Walk, shouting slurs at Jewish and Muslim students, calling women sluts for having exposed shoulders, and following people who were ignoring him, what I realized was that the people who tell you that, in a lot of cases, just don't want the responsibility of what comes along with identifying yourself as being pro-feminist, pro-LGBT, or pro-equality. Ideology in name, not in action.

What I learned that day when I said "I'm transgender, fuck you!" was that centrists don't want to confront bullies because they can't play both sides of the equation when that happens, especially if they're not the target of said bullying. They wouldn't want to be next on the bullying list, would they? If they're seen as being complicit with trans people, they just might be the next target on the protest list, right? Better make sure the hate preacher's rights to harass students who aren't demonstrating is protected.

Yet when he came back and some of us went to counter-protest him again, we were escorted away by school security. His First Amendment rights were protected. Ours were denied. Don't worry, though, they had therapy dogs and coloring books available.

Many leaders in the supposedly monolithic atheist community have been the same way. They're all for the equal rights of women, ethnic and racial minorities, and LGBT people (or at least LGB), but were more than willing to say that there were problems on both sides when it came down to taking a side.

When cisgender straight white men threw us under the bus after the election, we were called bullies for daring to disagree, and told that there were bigger problems than us right now.

Then, as each month passed, trans rights were taken away by this government, Nazis and white supremacists were emboldened and motivated, and views like "feminism is a mental illness" were platformed.

I would say they became popular, but these were by no means new ideas, even within the community itself.

In the last year since coming out publicly, I've published four books, started five podcasts, and traveled the country speaking to different groups of people about my experience. I've interviewed as many different kinds of people as I possibly could; not just about trans issues and visibility, but about trying to survive in the face of two relatively harmful theaters of experience.

We knew where the bigots stood. We knew where the racists stood. We knew where the bullies stood. But those who identified themselves as feminists and allies in rhetoric were more than ready to play the "both sides are just as bad" game when it came time to actually take a stand and defend those ideas.

Whether it was because they didn't like SJWs, because they thought feminism wasn't really necessary anymore, or because sometimes people in the affected groups weren't nice enough about it, they weren't willing to stand up for those ideas when the cards were on the table.

It's like how we trans people get accused of alienating allies when we call out harmful behavior. Supposed allies are really quick to hold their allyship over our heads and accuse us of alienating them for something as simple as reminding them of our pronouns, or asking them not to use a certain word.

The administration at my school said they defended and protected us, yet the very last thing to happen to me as a student on that campus was being followed into the bathroom and harassed by a security guard. While having a friend with me, after saying my name and identity, and after showing my ID, I was still commanded to prove my own identity in the bathroom because "Marissa might be a gender neutral name."

This was ten minutes after I sat through the LGBT Center graduation ceremony where the university's gender identity-inclusive policy was bragged about for being so forward and being so present early in the game, comparatively. At a ceremony where I spoke because I wasn't going to attend any other graduation ceremonies, I was harassed in the bathroom by an employee of the university for the crime of using the bathroom on the way to my car.

Feminism Theater is claiming to hold feminist ideals, but then also telling feminists that they're just as bad as misogynists when confronted with a conversation between the two.

Feminism Theater is believing in inclusivity, but telling groups fighting for their identities and lives that they need to wait their turn when they're speaking up for themselves.

Feminism Theater is having the right ideas, but believing that it's enough to just have the ideas, rather than supporting them.

Feminism Theater is being anti-rape, anti-harassment, anti-discrimination, but immediately blaming the victim when someone speaks up about a leader in the movement, someone who shares their experience of those traumatic events with a #MeToo tag, or who isn't willing to ignore the inappropriate advances of a man who has been told "no."

Feminism Theater is hero worship when someone in a movement is accused of acting inappropriately, and harassing the people who came forward to expose the acts or defend those who did.

Feminism Theater is performative allyship.

Being an ally isn't about saying the right things or having the right thoughts. It's about standing up and confronting those with harmful opinions or actions when push comes to shove. It's about listening instead of talking over someone sharing their experience or telling you what they need.

If recent posts of #MeToo have you thinking that most of these people just probably made up their experience and are doing it to be trendy or to get attention, you're part of the problem.

This weekend, I attended an atheist/humanist convention in Philadelphia. I brought my books with me and had a merchandise table. I listened to speakers from many different backgrounds share their experience, ideals, and advice. I interacted with these speakers and the other attendees of the conference.

Outside of someone deciding that moving my stuff off a table and claiming it as their own was an appropriate thing to do, nothing was upsetting about this conference. Nobody was shouted down. Nobody was called slurs. Nobody was told that their identity was a mental illness. I wasn't told to go away or to sit down because I wasn't important enough to be there right now, and neither was Callie Wright.

Yet more than one person there has been accused of harassment or sexual assault.

Nobody said anything about that, either.

FROM SHITLORD TO SJW
CHRISTOPHER REED

W hen someone would rattle off labels to me, I used to shrug them off. "Oh, I guess that makes me a pro-LGBT-rights, cis-hetero male shitlord anti-feminist." But at least for some time, I really was.

My drug of choice was (and still is, for the most part) YouTube. The channels I subscribed to consisted of YouTube atheism's greatest minibosses like TJ Kirk, Armoured Skeptic, Thunderfoot, Karen Straughan, and even the destroyer of Mythicist Milwaukee 2017 himself, Sargon of Akkad.

I watched these channels like they would be taken down at any time. Reveling in the mud-flinging toward the screeching leftist, third-wave feminists was a spectator sport for me at this shameful time in my life. The good news is that I wasn't to remain this trilby-wearing, euphoric, neckbearded atheist for long. Big changes were coming my way.

The Red Pill was never in my future; I always thought that these folks using a plot device from a somewhat diversely cast film from the 90s directed by two transfolk to explain if you're in or out of the anti-fem agenda was a bit striking, to say the least. People rarely think of what's said, where it came from, and why it means what it means, and with the written and spoken word, *words have meanings*.

The tightrope that I was walking led to two outcomes. One was a plunge into an abyss that would have me shirk my empathy and lead me down a path to becoming a worthless internet troll teetering on nihilism. And the other, more narrow path—the one that actually would take effort on my part; the one that would have me stumble with every step forward; the one that has led to me being who I am today.

My path is focused, my efforts measured, and my mind more at ease than it's been in a long time... at least until I go to Twitter.

I didn't see my blind spots then, and like many folks in this world who want to think that they're good allies (not how it works) and that they are so very woke (don't ever use that term to describe yourself), the real truth is that you have so very, very far to go before you get anywhere close to being either.

At one time I used to laugh at the third-wave feminists, the social justice warriors, the crowd of college-age "intellectuals" that at the time I felt were pushing for censorship. They were all prey to the media I consumed, and I lapped it up like someone who just spilled single malt on the hardwood flooring.

Watching how people got "triggered" (even though at the time I had no idea that using a term like that was wholly inappropriate to describe what was really going on) filled me with a sense of satisfaction that would be hard for me to place a finger on these days. I'd say that Richard Spencer getting clocked would be close, but I'm still working on myself.

It wasn't until more than a year had passed before I

started to come to the realization that people like me were being assholes for no good reason, and not using even a smidge of empathy to see life from the perspective of those who were protesting or speaking out. I was a shitlord.

For many, becoming a better person, getting involved in activism, and starting to develop a sense of the world that exists outside of the walls of their skulls, isn't a goal.

There are a multitude of people in the "facts-not-feels" atheist movement who are perfectly content with getting the answer to whether we have sufficient evidence that a god or gods exist right and stopping there. I know all of this because I was that person. I just *knew* that atheist rights were the most important thing to fight for, the most righteous battle in which I could be a standard bearer.

How supremely wrong I was!

There were quite a few people within the atheist movement who helped lead me out of the pit by simply teaching me indirectly (podcasts are magic in this regard) that the same reason I was an LGBTQ rights activist, even though I was not a member of that community, could be applied to feminism not being just for women (I know the arguments against this too)—it is also good for men, as it will help dissolve the patriarchy and break the rigid gender role structure that we set up for some fucking reason.

It was probably at that point that I started actually listening to what feminists had to say, and little by little, the world started making more sense through that lens. I was being incessantly mean to people who had the interests of people outside of their own cliques in mind. I was being such an asshole... Of course the pay gap exists, of course women scientists have a harder time in college, of course women stay quiet about sexual assault because of how rape culture is a thing *literally* everywhere.

I do want to go back a bit. I realized that I did seem to

agree with a lot of problematic statements, and reminding myself of them makes me shudder at how I supported them at any point in my life.

I was brought up as a Baptist Christian youth from the South who was around casual racism most of my childhood, and had a very-much-into-athletics dad who'd also served in the military and flirted with becoming a member of a militia in the early 90s during the Clinton era... because the liberals were going to be coming for our guns any day now.

Any day—no, really, any day since 1992, just like Christ coming back any day now.

I recall have heard the word "nigger" on many, many, many occasions growing up, as my extended family were all from rural Arkansas and grew up in the pre-integration Civil Rights era. I'm not making excuses for them using that word —it's reprehensible regardless of context—but as a child, I never understood what that meant.

Kids aren't stupid, so I knew that it was a derogatory statement my family used against people of color, but it was nothing I would ever use, and for good reason. I could never be *that* kind of racist. Sure, I had to work my way through the mistrust of people of color that was etched into me by my parents and extended family. I'd be wrong to suggest that I never exhibited *any* problematic behavior; you did just read a whole lot of me being a shitlord to women, right?

I was a kid of a military parent. I saw firsthand how PTSD could fuck up relationships between spouses, and especially parents and their kids. However, growing up in the military, you learn really quick how to slide in and out of social situations, keep ideas to yourself, and essentially make friends with anyone of any race/gender/religion because it's about survival in the schoolyard, and most of us were pretty used to uprooting our lives every couple of years.

I've had to be a social chameleon for so long that the identity that made me "me" had to be pushed way down inside. Call it a coping mechanism or an excuse, but for a good portion of my life, I had felt like I had to be callous, I had to be hyper-masculine, and I had to be someone who used irony and satire to mask the person who really wanted to do what the girls were doing, not because I was a girl, but because I disliked most of the macho/manly activities.

I love my mom for this. She knew from a pretty early age that I was different. Not special, mind you—we're all special —but different from the binary, and she was okay with that.

Before being properly institutionalized in schools and churches, I recall wearing her clothes for dress up, learning how to do "girly" things (ugh, I hate that word), and learning how to do what my mom did around the house—like the cleaning and cooking, as I grew up in a pretty chauvinistic household.

She treated me as the daughter of the family, of which I was originally supposed to be, and trust me, I've heard about it all my life. In many ways, I am that daughter to her. I'll have to revisit this someday once I figure out my own brain's inner workings. Seriously, who gets to their mid-thirties with identity problems, right?!

One trait about myself I knew I needed to work on was my deficient sense of empathy. It's something we all need to have more of, but rarely do we learn how to develop it. For me, it was the years and years spent with fingers in my ears, and my white privilege pinned to my chest with a "lalalalalala, I can't hear you" attitude, coupled with an "I've had a hard life too!" perspective, that kept me from actually sitting down and listening to people and their stories.

This is where the shitlord in me started to die a slow death. I had listened to gay people in the past, trans people, bi people, everyone under the rainbow, really... Why had I not listened to anyone else? Why was I mocking people for telling me to check my privilege? Why did I think that feminism was a cancer? Was I one of the baddies?

Then someone cracked the façade of my cognitive dissonance so deftly, so simply, that I can recall the moment like it was yesterday. In an interview with AronRa, someone had asked him if he was a feminist. I chuckled to myself, "There's no way that AronRa is a feminist, no way at all."

Then it happened. He said he was.

"Wait, what?!?" I thought, and thankfully the video I was watching had someone push further for clarification. Weren't feminists the ones mad at video games? Weren't feminists the ones pushing for censorship on college campuses? Weren't feminists the ones who'd take a fun thing and turn it into a thought control mound of gray clay?

AronRa had simply said he was a feminist, but I couldn't figure out how, and it was simple. He played to something I had already defined for myself: I can be straight-ish and still be a supporter of LGBTQ rights, right? Then I could be a man and support equality between the sexes.

"Wait, that's not feminism, that's gender egalitarianism!"

The back of my mind chimed in, "Asshole, if feminism isn't about female dominance and misandry, you've got a lot of apologizing to do."

Oh.

Oh...

Fuck me!

It wasn't right there on the spot that I changed, but the ball had been put into play, and it would never be put back. I learned what others had been trying to tell me for years—that the culture we celebrate as amazing is built off a system that has kept women down, kept "out groups" marginalized, and ultimately built rigid rules for gender and pressed flesh into them until they conformed or broke.

It was sobering.

Days turned into weeks, and I found myself killing my idols. I unsubscribed to channel after channel after hearing them frame their hate the wrong way for probably the millionth time before I put on my new ears. I started looking at the channels that were the targets of the hate and found myself actually learning something. My view from the window in my mind went from one facing a brick wall with a giant phallus on it to seeing writ large the words behind it that said, "You don't know half of what you think you know."

I was no longer avoiding the Black Lives Matter podcast segments. I was not ignoring women and people of color yelling at the world that the system I was propping up was killing them, was taking their freedoms away, and was worst of all ambivalent to their strife. I no longer laughed at having "privilege." It wasn't funny anymore. My game of life had been set on easy while everyone else was playing on legendary. I was a phony.

So how the fuck can I help fix this? Do people need my help?

I can use my platform to signal boost, I can use my troll powers for good, I can... I can...

I can help!

I'm in no measure perfect, as none of us are. Hell, I hope none of us ever try to be, because it's something you can't attain. But at the very least, we can try to be better to each other. We can attempt to lift others out of situations that weren't their fault. We can listen to each other and learn what life is like through someone else's eyes.

I'm still learning and will probably be as imperfect in my old age as I am now, because as much as we want to stay relevant and stay on top of things, this world has a way of letting the spotlight shine on you and your generation only for a brief time before it's onto the next generation for their turn.

What will we hand off to them? Will it be more of the patriarchal binaries and toxic roles we force upon them, or will we finally raze it all to the ground and plant anew in its ashes?

A REFLECTION ON #METOO

MARISSA ALEXA MCCOOL

Now that the viral nature of the #MeToo campaign has somewhat died down, I think it's important to take a look at this moment in time and analyze both what has happened and what we've learned from the recent discussion about sexual harassment and assault.

Once the campaign was reignited (not created) by Alyssa Milano, people everywhere began to respond to the hashtag in a variety of ways, and like anything women talk about on the Internet, it didn't come without its consequences, both positive and negative.

First, let's take a look at some of the positive effects, despite this conversation surrounding an extremely negative topic in and of itself.

The movement quickly became inclusive of other identities, more or less. Granted, this isn't a blanket statement. The original post specified women, saying that if all the women who had ever experienced sexual harassment or assault posted the phrase or hashtag "me too," that perhaps people would get an idea of just how big of a problem this actually is.

However, as with most posts that talk about the experience of women, almost immediately there was a "what about men?" response.

Ari Stillman of the SJW Circle-Jerk podcast brought up a great point of people presenting femme, whether they be cis women, trans women, non-binary or gender-nonconforming people who expressed any kind of femininity, or cis men who dared do anything feminine always having a target on them for it, and therefore the term being changed from women to people was helpful in illuminating the constant indictment of femininity in this society.

I will state for the record that I had no problem with men using this hashtag to tell their stories too. My issues with how some men responded will be for a later portion of this essay, but if we are to address these issues of assault and harassment, it is important to highlight that men are often ignored, laughed at, or bullied for even the thought of coming forward about their incidents of these experiences, and that's part of the problem too.

Overall, though, I saw people of all genders, all ages, all identities, all races, all sexualities, and all economic classes either telling their stories in detail, or just responding that they too had experienced this trauma on some level. That is a unity that we don't often see in societies and communities heavy on gatekeeping.

Some people (who weren't assholes) were motivated to change their behavior, or at least become aware of the behavior of others, due to the sheer amount of people using this hashtag.

This also isn't an indictment of straight cis white men, but it was alarming to see so many of them, many of whom are activists and/or public figures, respond with sheer surprise of how many posts they were seeing including this hashtag. On some level, I envy the idea that they could live in this world among this many women and not be aware of how many of their fellow community members had experienced harassment and assault. However, ignorance isn't bliss, and not knowing there is a problem isn't justification for a lack of action.

I don't know and can't say how many people will take actual action because of this hashtag, directly or indirectly, but I can say with some level of confidence that I think many more cis straight men gained a greater perspective on not just what people deal with, but how many of them have. We still do live in a world where women are seen as emotional, illogical, and irrational, and therefore it takes men vouching and speaking out about it as well before something is taken seriously.

A great level of empathy and bonding took place between many people who thought they were alone.

One of the most terrifying aspects of experiencing harassment and assault (and by the way, #MeToo), is the isolating feeling of having to prove yourself. Everyone around you seems ready to question anything, from if you were telling the truth to what you were wearing, to what you did to cause it to why you didn't avoid it, to why you didn't just leave.

Whether it be friends, police officers, administrators, or otherwise, the burden of proof is often immediately placed on the person who experienced these traumas. It's no wonder that people have such a hard time coming forward about what happened to them when they're almost instantly disbelieved and/or blamed for something that wasn't their fault.

If you ever want to gather an idea of how often this can happen, I recommend reading *We Believe You: Survivors of Campus Sexual Assault Speak Out* by Annie E. Clark and Andrea L. Pino. It was shortly before the #MeToo campaign that I was reading this book and saw a scenario that seemed really familiar. Like, scarily familiar.

The victim was a trans woman, like me. The victim went to school for their freshman year at Temple University in 2013, Temple being in Philadelphia, the same city that I transferred to for four-year when I went to UPenn.

When I got to the end of the story, I went back and checked the name of the author of this particular piece, and realized not only was it someone I knew, but it was someone with whom I went to the same community college, worked on the student newspaper, and had at least one class. They knew me before I came out as trans, so it was difficult to immediately go to this person and say anything, but that's how small these worlds can be.

While the sage advice is often to never read the comments, I can say the case with at least a majority percentage of the ones I saw was that other people were either sharing their own story or expressing love and support for the person who posted it. Those are the sentiments people desperately need when they experience trauma, and I was thrilled for those in my community who weren't isolated and exiled for speaking out and were instead embraced.

Now that we've had three positive things to talk about, it's time to talk about the negative consequences of this campaign, and of course I mean other than that so many people have been sexually harassed or assaulted.

The phrase was co-opted, mocked, refuted, or written off; either for reasons of disbelief, general shitholetry, changing the narrative, or victim blaming.

When some men realized that the women were speaking about something men as a class were responsible for, some of them engaged in a particular behavior I like to call NotAlling. This started back a few years ago when women were using the hashtag #YesAllWomen, and men responded with #NotAllMen.

The general problem with this behavior is that it changes a conversation to make it about you, personally, and is often used not to continue or extend conversations, but to shut them down.

For instance, NotAlling with both campaigns often brought up, "What about men who deal with it?" "What about prison?" and other male-centric concerns, and while these are all legitimate issues, it becomes questionable when the only time someone mentions these things is when they see women speaking about their own experience. If you only use those examples to stop conversations and shut women up, you don't actually care about them. It's like responding with "What about homeless veterans?" in response to taking in refugees, but then never actually doing anything to help homeless veterans.

Only using a stance of self-righteousness to stop people from trying to speak out or help others isn't helpful, and is only designed to relieve you of any guilt from actions you may have taken to contribute to this problem, and it's a hell of a lot easier to assume that everyone else is lying and it's not your fault, while at the same time getting to sit on your moral pedestal, than it is to listen to people, learn something, and consider your own potential involvement in this behavior.

Sometimes it was using the laughter reaction when people said it, or placing it on a pair of socks. Or some people of all genders responded with a modified tag of #NotMeEither, or some variant of that, because of course their anecdotal experience is always congruent with reality. "I didn't experience this; therefore, it doesn't happen."

I don't quite know where people using #IHave fit in to this analysis, but to once again refer to Ari's episode of SJWCJ, it does in some ways change the narrative, make the conversation about you, and expect getting a pat on the back for knowing that you've participated in this behavior and were public about it. If you're only owning up to problematic things you've done to be commended for your honesty and never actually change anything, that's worthy of distrust and wariness.

The worst co-opting I saw, however, came in the form of some men using the hashtag to correct the conversation. I saw it shared in both post and meme form where it said something along the lines of "financial abuse and sexual neglect" were the real problems, thus putting the onus back on women and also claiming victimhood for putting nice coins in a woman and sex not falling out—not to mention equating that with, or positioning it as the superior problem to, women talking about abuse, harassment, and assault.

This mentality is often seen in the "But I'm a nice guy/But the friendzone" aspect of relationships where someone feels entitled to sex because they paid attention to their person of interest, bought them things in hopes of getting laid, or believe that they've been friendzoned—that is, relegated to the status of "friend" rather than "romantic partner," which is apparently some sort of crime.

Not only are these mentalities celebrated, but they're defended when a man goes on a shooting spree and murders women for not accepting his advances.

So while it was no surprise to see this campaign being co-opted in the ways it was, it doesn't make that colonization of the issue any less harmful.

Some people still believe that victims of harassment and assault deserve it.

"What were you wearing?"

"Why were you out so late?"

"How much did you have to drink?"

"Did you lead him on?"

"Boys will be boys."

"Why weren't you at home making dinner for your husband?"

(That particular one was thrown at a woman who had to respond with "I was eight.")

Never mind the gender roles and implication of fault belonging to the woman for not behaving as that man believed she should; this also highlights the idea that "if this happened, she must've caused it or it was otherwise her fault."

Once again, it is a hell of a lot easier to assume the victim did something to deserve it and wipe it from your mind than to express empathy for another human being. It's easier to think they must've lied about it than to listen to a traumatic recounting of events. It's also easier to commit such actions and say that your victim deserved it rather than check your behavior.

I think of the men who put up such a fuss about behavior policies being put into place at conventions, and thinking that not harassing or assaulting people meant nobody could flirt or have sex anymore. The same ideas are perpetuated when finding out that there are secret networks of women who discuss having been assaulted by leaders in their communities, and how they are afraid to come out about it lest they be exiled, blamed, doxxed, harassed, bullied, trolled, and/or sued for speaking out.

If the idea of women talking about the behavior of men to each other bothers you, maybe you're worried about them talking about *your* behavior. That should tell you something.

Of course you can flirt with people at a convention. But if they say no, it stops there.

Of course you can have sex with someone at a convention (preferably in the hotel room and not on the conference floor). But if they don't consent to this, that's where it becomes not okay.

Consent is mandatory, and ignoring that is what leads to many of the stories seen represented by this hashtag and campaign.

It still takes dozens of people speaking out for people to take allegations seriously.

One of the biggest reasons that sex crimes go unreported, in addition to all the gatekeeping and questioning mentioned earlier, is simply because victims don't think they'll be believed.

Think of how many celebrities or public figures in the last few years have been accused of rape, harassment, or assault, and immediately the hero worship brigades ride forth in the alleged perpetrator's defense. Whether it be a football coach, family-friendly comedian, movie producer, or candidate for President of the United States, the behavior is defended or dismissed as "locker room talk," "boys being boys," "it was a different time," or anything in between.

And when someone who openly brags about sexual assault gets elected to the highest office in the land, it's not exactly a sign of moving forward on this issue.

Overall, though, it does seem that more people of all genders felt empowered to speak out about their experiences, and a lot more people listened, perhaps for the first time. If there's a first step in turning this behavior from being something celebrated or disbelieved into something that makes people steer away from it, it's more people speaking up, speaking out, and simply saying, "I believe you."

Never underestimate the power of believing someone who tells you what they've experienced. It can save someone's life.

STAGE III

Bargaining

"Sacrifice is a form of bargaining."

—HOLBROOK JACKSON

MANAGING THE FIRE

MARISSA ALEXA MCCOOL

I 've never been good at resting.

At one point last year, I was suffering from pneumonia, yet I still had the urge and instinct to get stuff done. My husband practically sat on my chest and ordered me to lay back down. That's what it took to get me off my feet and not trying to do eight things at a time.

Maybe it's because I had it drilled into my head that working hard—through pain, exhaustion, and frustration—was the only way to be accepted, successful, and strong. A lot of it was unintentional I'm sure, but I felt growing up that anytime I needed a break or a day off that I was chastised for daring to think such things were acceptable.

Therefore, I find myself in the difficult position of desperately needing a break from the world being on fire, but every time I think I'm ready to cut things off for a while, this overwhelming sense of guilt takes over; shaming me for daring to even think of disengaging when silence can be interpreted as consent or compliance.

Speaking out does not come without its consequences,

and as much fun as it can be, and as great as the reciprocation can be, it doesn't come without its toll.

For instance, being on the trans rights activism front, it's only natural that I know other trans rights activists, and a lot of their posts often include the original source of someone saying something horrible about us.

Yes, it is often followed by a refutation, but taking in yet another person who doesn't think we're people or valid or in charge of our identity is taken in nonetheless, and it gets fucking exhausting to have to justify your humanity to yourself, even when being shown an example of someone else already doing that part. I internalize everything, and it's impossible for me to see the horrible thing consequence-free.

Combine that on the personal front with being hurt badly in successive days by people in my own life for anything from being dehumanized to shamed for needing some space, and it feels like the world is closing in on me. Like it's a New Age version of Mean World Syndrome, where instead of the media convincing me that everyone is going to get murdered, the people out there who find that action against us justified get their signals boosted constantly; and it seems unavoidable.

I needed to get away from it; that, and putting myself out there to only be called a thing or deadnamed or misgendered constantly, it wears on my already tired and weakened battery. Yet those who march against all marginalized groups and kill people with their cars to prove it don't sleep, and silence from white people can be seen as complicity.

That line becomes gray and hard to spot, and the right thing to do can be lost between trying to be there and visible and running on fumes, but feeling exhausted, defeated, ineffective, and in desperate need of recharge. I can only see how a majority of people think of me and my community so many times before I need to not see it for a while.

But again, that guilt runs deep. That sense of feeling like resting or needing a break is giving up; it keeps the candles burning late and the car running past the E. It's an internal vicious circle of horrible, self-defeating inner monologues.

In the midst of feeling myself hitting another low, I took another self-imposed social media ban, barely a week after spending the weekend in Seattle with my partner the same way. Taking it a step further, though, I deleted Facebook and Twitter from my phone entirely, following in the footsteps of someone I dearly love, Eli Bosnick. Though not for the same reason, he's someone else who puts himself out there boldly, and deals with the blowback as best he can. Yet like the rest of us, he remains human and can only deal with so much negativity and horrible hatred in human behavior.

Sometimes it's just about learning that the fire doesn't always need to be put out immediately, but left to be managed by allies who step up in your place. You know, like real allies who aren't in it for the cookie.

Recording my own podcast tonight, I found myself breaking down at the end while discussing a somewhat traumatic recent event, and I had to ask my cohost if they could edit the show. I couldn't even bring myself to deal with it on that level anymore. I needed escape from the world; into the arms of my husband, my partners, the innocent eyes of my kids who have no idea the kind of negativity from which I truly try to shield them ...

And yet I can't stop feeling like a failure for it. Nor can I stop feeling one when the next transphobic asshole thinks they're being original with whatever apologetic they heard from someone else and thought it was brilliant.

I need to fight all I can, especially for those who aren't in a position to do so, but I'm not in a good headspace at all. Things are getting to me, and even in writing this post with no intention of reading the comments, I'm stuck between keeping it to myself and fearing pointlessness. Or posting it and feeling pointlessness.

Maybe for a while, I need to let the other firefighters take a shift. I've been on the call for far too long. But if something is lost in the fire when I'm not there, I'll never stop blaming myself.

So be it. I'm no good to anyone with a dead battery.

CRISIS OF FAITH

TONY OPELT

W hen I was in high school, I had two amazing friends
—my best friends, Nik and Rollin. I have countless
fond memories of the three of us hanging out throughout
that period of our lives, and I'll never forget any of them.
Those years made me who I am today, for the most part.

I was a nerdy kid, living in a small town called Neillsville
in the state of Wisconsin with a population of less than
3,000. There was never anything interesting going on in that
town—we always had to drive to either Marshfield or Eau
Claire to do anything exciting.

Still, we found ways to keep ourselves busy. Mainly, that
involved playing video games. I couldn't even say how many
hours we put into playing *Super Smash Bros.* or *Mario Kart*, but
playing games on the GameCube was our drug of choice.

We also spent a lot of time making videos. We would
write, direct, and act in our own short sketch comedy videos
and show them off to our friends and families. We were so
proud of them, even the stupid ones that didn't really work.

In fact, the summer after we graduated, we worked on a
huge project—filming a bunch of new sketches and editing

them into a half-hour short film. It took up much of our free time, but it was our proudest moment when we premiered it for our friends at an end-of-summer party.

Then came college. Unfortunately for the three of us, we each decided on going to different universities. Nik went to UW Green Bay, Rollin to UW Madison, and I went to Martin Luther College in New Ulm, MN.

I suppose this is the proper time to mention that I was (and still am) a devout Christian. I wanted to attend a Christian university with my desired degree being in education. At the time, I was completely unaware of how poor of a fit this college was for me, but I was mainly happy to be away from my hometown and out on my own.

My entire life, I had been brought up to believe in the standard Christian beliefs, but along with those came a lot of bigotry and hate toward "the gays," as my congregation called them. I wouldn't say that I hated them or harbored any ill will toward them, but I was wary of them. At that time in my life, that was simply what I was told was the right thing to do. My college of choice fit right in with those beliefs.

My friends and I stayed in touch through instant messenger apps, things no one even uses these days. We also used Facebook—something that only college students used at the time because it was so new. This was back when you had to have a college email address in order to sign up and make an account. We didn't like being far apart, and we certainly didn't like waiting for the holidays to roll around to see each other again, but we dealt with it as best we could.

There was a particular night that I'll never forget. I had just finished chatting with Nik when Rollin struck up a conversation with me on one of the messaging apps we used. It was the usual fare—talking about classes, video games, and other random stuff just so we didn't have to stop talking.

Rollin asked me when I would be home next so he could

talk to me in person about something. I wasn't sure, and I remember badgering him for what was so important that he wanted to talk to me in person about it. I'm sure I wasn't the nicest guy in that moment. I had a horrible curiosity for when people knew something I didn't.

I eventually started guessing what it was about—a death in the family, medical issues, and any other horrible thing I could think of.

It was at this exact moment that some memories came flooding back—memories of various people in my family wondering if Rollin was gay. So I asked him if he was gay. The seconds between that question and Rollin's answer felt like an eternity.

Yes.

He clarified afterward that he was bisexual and not simply gay, but the "Yes" stuck with me the most. I had a crisis of conscience at that moment. I loved my friend—he was truly closer to a brother than a friend to me, along with Nik. I had no idea what to do because my church and college both said that being gay was a sin and a horrible offense. I had two options—love my friend, or love my church.

I chose my friend.

I don't remember my exact words to him regarding my response to this news, but I do remember praising him for his bravery, thanking him for his honesty, and assuring him that his faith and trust in me was not misplaced. He was still the same person he always was. I just knew him a little better now, was all.

Looking back on all of this, it still makes me feel ashamed that it took a personal experience for me to realize that there's nothing wrong with anyone in the LGBTQ community—that they're just people trying to live their lives. I wish it hadn't taken such a drastic moment to make me realize this, but often, a drastic moment is exactly what people need to realize when they're wrong about something.

Several years later, Rollin and I both stood up in Nik's wedding. Rollin and Nik will stand up in my wedding (my fiancée is really excited about it), and I know that Nik and I will stand up in Rollin's wedding if he ever decides to marry his current boyfriend. They're really cute together, and they're great for each other.

I left that university after that semester because of their policy against the LGBTQ community, and I left my church after that. I found a new church that proudly accepts anyone, regardless of gender identity or sexual orientation, because its primary message is "Love God, Love People," which is exactly what I believe.

It's good to know that there are churches out there that do not hate and are inclusive to everyone. You'll find them if you look for them, and more of them are coming around to that line of thinking every day.

I still miss my friends. Nik still lives in Green Bay while Rollin moved to California and is living with his boyfriend. I live in Minnesota now, so seeing Nik happens every now and then, but it's rare that I get to see Rollin, and that's a shame because without him, I wouldn't be who I am today. He has, perhaps, been the biggest influence in my life, and he is singlehandedly responsible for bringing about the biggest change to my character.

And I couldn't be happier about it.

SENSES

MARISSA ALEXA MCCOOL

Thunder crashing around my ears in the form of a heartfelt laugh in my direction.

The sun outshines the brightest star directly in my field of vision, causing the squint to be my natural state of being.

Every person could be a danger to me, as they have eyes, and those eyes could drift to me and bring upon the worst and most paranoid of my expectations.

The world is too loud, and ugliness is too disheartening. Today, I can't escape the casualty list of its ravages.

TITLE GOES HERE
KIMBERLY ELEANOR PANNELL

M y real name is Kimberly Eleanor Pannell.
I specify "real" because I'm certain there are those of you who have known me only under a pseudonym, and may continue your relationship with me under a pseudonym at some point in the future. I have a variety of reasons for this, as many of those who use pseudonyms do, but for me it has largely to do with my desire to have an identity separate from my "real" one, or that which my friends and family have always known me under, for exploring "who I really am" in the online space that is social media—or, specifically as it has been for me for the past few years, Facebook.

I met Marissa under my real name, before I realized that Marissa, while indeed being her own real name, was not the name she was given at birth. Nor was "female" the gender she was assigned at birth, though that does not and never has and never will make it any less her own.

This has been and will be, as I have come to realize, a recurring theme in my journey of self-discovery since drifting away and severing my ideological ties from the religion and belief system in which I was raised, and in which most of my family still reside: The idea that each individual person to ever walk this Earth is ultimately in charge of deciding who they truly are, though throughout history many have been denied this freedom through such oppressive systems as those built under religion, or simply predicated under misogyny, tradition, and fear of the different or the unknown.

I first began questioning my own belief system at around the age of sixteen—or at least, at the time, I thought it was my own. I would later discover that it was only ever truly a belief system which was fed to me and reinforced through a conditioning system of fear, threats, and unfulfilled promises.

I was attending my parents' church's school at the time—a school built exclusively for the purpose of educating church members' children and keeping them, thusly, locked away from "outside influences" which could turn them away from the faith (these "outside influences," I would quickly realize, mostly consisted of anything that could be considered real science or psychology.)

This was a tumultuous time in my life—I had always been an incredibly insecure girl; my insecurities hinging largely on my crooked smile, which my parents both lacked the economic feasibility to fix, and the integrity to see that barring your child from getting braces was not any great insult to "God's design."

However, no matter how great these insecurities were, they were soon eclipsed by the greatest existential threat I had ever faced—the cognitive dissonance I encountered when I realized, gradually and yet somehow, at the same time, all at once, that I truly was "smarter" than God.

How could this be so? How could I even entertain such a blasphemous thought?

Well, those who still advocate for some form of religion, or spirituality, or faith will say that it is only the fault of the particular belief system in which I was raised. I am perfectly content to allow them to believe this. I cannot, however, in good conscience, agree.

My first "real" job, out of high school, was at a history and government museum in downtown Philadelphia. I had had many odd jobs before then—hot dog cart worker, newspaper delivery person, general courier, babysitter, sandwich shop employee—though these had all been positions for which I was paid under the table.

This museum job I got through the recommendation of another employee there, who had started off in the position she was recommending me for and then later elevated to the administration staff. She had gone to my school, a few grades ahead.

Here, after about a year—my memory is terrible with dates, so it was most likely a little under—a new boy started showing up. I remember trying to decide if I thought he was cute or not—and eventually landing on "yes."

However, after he started making polite conversation with me (to my great confusion) when we were posted in the same areas at the same time, and eventually friended me on Facebook, I soon discovered he was in a relationship. Disappointed though I was at this confirmation, it wasn't as if I was greatly surprised, or had ever expected him to return the crush.

Nevertheless, he still kept in contact with me, both online and through the number he gave me, and though my religious upbringing told me to find this odd, I knew, logically, that it was a fairly normal practice. He was never anything but polite and respectful to me. So much so that when he asked, during one conversation that I likely initiated under some amount of stress, if "everything was all right," a floodgate opened in me and I found myself entrusting him with greater and greater confessions, larger and more intimate portraits of my soul.

Much has changed since then. I eventually admitted to the crush, though I knew nothing would come of it. He is now in a happy and long-lasting relationship with a different woman than who I initially saw on his Facebook profile. In my head, I am happy for him, though feelings as strong as the ones I had, and hatched under the circumstances I was in, sometimes never truly go away.

He never did cut off contact with me, despite my urgings and insistences of how much of a burden I "knew I was," and how hard it was for me to "break the habit." He did stop replying to my messages for the greater part after a while, preoccupied with his own life and the people who take precedence in it.

So here, in a series of patchwork snapshots, is an idea of the kind of self-discovery and reflection—and yes, even healing—that can take place when you truly become comfortable with someone, regardless of whatever label could objectively be prescribed to your relationship. I don't know how many of these messages he's ever read. I hope it's all of them, but even if it's none, I can still say that the very act of sharing them has brought me something resembling catharsis, or at least the start of it.

A note: Names have been changed to protect the identities of those referenced herein.

JUNE 2ND, 12:48 A.M.

Today was my little sister's graduation.
    Okay, actually yesterday, at this point.
    I hadn't been in that church in a while.
    I don't know. It was weird.
    Bittersweet.

Like remembering who I was for brief patches of time.

Remembering what it's like to love people.

People you grew up with. People you've been through things with.

I still hate The Universe Without God. It's lonely. And cold. And empty. Not necessarily because of his absence, but because I've lost the ways in which I used to identify myself and other people, and *with* other people.

Idk. I'm probably feeling sorry for myself. Again. Just felt like venting to someone because I'm actually feeling feelings other than anger and confusion tonight. A little bit of confusion, maybe. But mostly bittersweet nostalgia. A little heartache. Longing, maybe, for things I already know are impossible to ever have again.

I hope you've been well. I want to tell you again, while I'm still in a clear frame of mind, how much I respect you, not only for putting up with all of my nonsense and feelings of entitlement to your life, but for what you do.

You're good people. Better people than me. I'm really lucky to have known you, even if we never talk again. Goodnight, Andrews. Take care of yourself.

❀

JUNE 24TH, 3:31 A.M.

So there are certain humans in my life that are under the impression that I am into women.

And I am too tired to argue with them.

Also, I don't know if they're wrong.

Because due to circumstances beyond my control, I haven't been "into" anyone for the last few years.

But I have half-seriously, half-not, mentioned that if anyone fits a lot of the lesbian stereotypes, it's me.

Bookworm, awkward, never dated in high school, avoid going out.

"Too smart" for men.

Funny (at least to me).

And like, not gonna lie, it's really nice to have women hit on you.

There's one on my friends list who lives in like, Germany, who's super smart and super pretty who's been hardcore flirty on more than one occasion.

And if she lived closer I probably would have been like "fuck it, Anna. Hit me with your best shot. At least neither one of us is getting pregnant."

But it's made me seriously ponder the question of, how far would my parents go to "accept" me.

My mom, for sure, would lose her shit.

My dad would be less theatrical, but probably still have a lot of reservations about it.

I would be one of few lesbians to ever emerge from that place.

I actually can't think of any in my lifetime, but there has to have been at least one or two in the history of the school; it's been around for a while.

There has been more than one male student to come out as gay once he's made a safe distance from the place.

So this would be like, the most feminist thing I could possibly do.

And it's hilarious to think of the double standards that this would reveal, and just how fucked up people's priorities are in the name of prejudice.

"You're into vaginas? There is a place in the deepest pit of hell reserved for you."

"You had a baby out of wedlock? At least you like dick!"

And it would be like, the saving grace for my older sister's reputation.

She eloped with a guy she'd met four months earlier and my mom found out from someone else.

But if Kim enjoyed playing the clituar...

I would be, like, the permanent black sheep of the Pannell family.

It would be quite a way to burn my bridges with that place.

"You remember that really smart Pannell girl? She makes out with chicks now. No, not ironically."

I feel like there's a lot of material here, but I'm too sleep-deprived to mine it for all it's worth.

But I felt like you would enjoy that much, at least.

Goodnight. Or morning.

JUNE 25TH, 1:30 A.M.

So there are certain humans in my life that are under the impression that I am into women.

And I am too tired to argue with them.

Also, I don't know if they're wrong.

Because due to circumstances beyond my control, I haven't been "into" anyone for the last few years.

But I have half-seriously, half-not, mentioned that if anyone fits a lot of the lesbian stereotypes, it's me.

Bookworm, awkward, never dated in high school, avoid going out.

"Too smart" for men.

Funny (at least to me).

And like, not gonna lie, it's really nice to have women hit on you.

There's one on my friends list who lives in like, Germany, who's super smart and super pretty who's been hardcore flirty on more than one occasion.

And if she lived closer I probably would have been like "fuck it, Anna. Hit me with your best shot. At least neither one of us is getting pregnant."

But it's made me seriously ponder the question of, how far would my parents go to "accept" me.

My mom, for sure, would lose her shit.

My dad would be less theatrical, but probably still have a lot of reservations about it.

I would be one of few lesbians to ever emerge from that place.

I actually can't think of any in my lifetime, but there has to have been at least one or two in the history of the school; it's been around for a while.

There has been more than one male student to come out as gay once he's made a safe distance from the place.

So this would be like, the most feminist thing I could possibly do.

And it's hilarious to think of the double standards that this would reveal, and just how fucked up people's priorities are in the name of prejudice.

"You're into vaginas? There is a place in the deepest pit of hell reserved for you."

"You had a baby out of wedlock? At least you like dick!"

And it would be like, the saving grace for my older sister's reputation.

She eloped with a guy she'd met four months earlier and my mom found out from someone else.

But if Kim enjoyed playing the clituar...

I would be, like, the permanent black sheep of the Pannell family.

It would be quite a way to burn my bridges with that place.

"You remember that really smart Pannell girl? She makes out with chicks now. No, not ironically."

I feel like there's a lot of material here, but I'm too sleep-deprived to mine it for all it's worth.

But I felt like you would enjoy that much, at least.

Goodnight. Or morning.

JULY 11TH, 2:51 A.M.

You don't know how many times a day I want to just get it over with and fall asleep and not wake up before I get any more attached to anything or anyone and it becomes even harder all over again.

I wish I had been through all of the terrible things my friends have been through.

Because I'm already told I exaggerate, and I feel like this anyway.

Might as well be the scapegoat for everyone else who's apparently not exaggerating, and go out with a bang.

But you can't talk people into staying alive with that mindset, can you?

The last time I went to therapy was months ago, and it's because my dad found out I was talking about suicide on social media (whoops, big no-no) because somebody called him. I don't know who. And he paid for the session, because it's not that expensive, and also because apparently my life means something to him.

And other people; these "friends"—people from across the world that I've never met in person—were offering to help too, because there's a chance I might get off my ass and do something for other people someday, and that makes me worth an investment.

I rarely feel like I'll live up to that.

The reason kids romanticize suicide is poignancy. At least, that's the conclusion I came to a while ago. You don't get poignancy very often. But freak everyone out by saying nonexistence sounds more attractive than existence, and suddenly everyone around you becomes a Validation Machine, and you feel like you'll live forever.

The older you get the harder it becomes to romanticize it, and then when it's your turn to talk someone out of it, there's about an 80% chance you don't believe anything you're saying because it's the same bullshit you've heard a million times yourself.

Then it becomes, "I'm not a professional. Someone with a degree who's qualified to prescribe you medicine to fix whatever chemical imbalance is going on in your brain can help you much more than I can. But I'll stay on the line if you want to talk about something stupid."

Then it becomes "I really don't know what to say. I can't make you do or not do anything, but I'll listen."

Then it becomes "You have a point. Your feelings make sense. Your reasons are valid."

Then it becomes, in the back of your head "Well, shit. If you don't want to die alone, can we do it together?"

But you don't say it out loud.

But you want to.

JULY 11TH, 3:12 A.M.

So if I haven't made it abundantly clear before:

Every day feels like it could be my last day to some part of my mind.

Which is why so many of these messages are like damn suicide notes.

It's not intentional; I just believe the doomsday feelings more than anything else that goes on up there.

And it would appear, as with most things, that I'm not the only one.

Which ironically probably makes me one of the worst people to try to talk anyone out of anything.

For all that I have to say apparently I can't say anything that really matters.

AUGUST 28TH, 2:32 A.M.

I've been arranging "venting machines" to replace you. It's not been as easy as one might think. :)

There's one, Leah Elwood—she's been a teacher, she went to law school at Georgetown, the last time I talked to her she was talking about waiting on flies to come into the lab. Not files—flies. She was doing an experiment with fruit flies.

She's super smart, even if I haven't always agreed with all of her politics for as long as I've known her. And she's so fucking flattering—there are people whose praise mean more to you than others, whether or not you're willing to admit it to yourself or anyone else. Hearing an accomplished lawyer/scientist/etc. say that you're probably the smartest person in most of the rooms you walk into is humbling and uncomfortable.

I still don't really feel that's correct. I'm not going to argue the intelligence part, but "the real world" has taught me that I'm always less impressive than I think I am.

And you. You do things. And that has made me uncomfortable since I've known you. I can't seem to get my feet off the ground; I can't seem to connect my emotions to my sense of identity and purpose for the life of me again. But you, you do things. And I sit on my parents' couch, feeling things. Feeling too many things, too deeply. Inactively.

But hey, I'm "smart," so it's okay, right? I'm just "preserving my brain"? One day I'll use it for something important, something meaningful, something impactful, someday soon.

But when?

You embarrass me. I don't care how little you feel you've accomplished or will accomplish in life; currently, it's far more than I've ever done. And as much as I like to delude myself into thinking I'm just "waiting for the right moment," that life is meaningless and we all die anyway, I haven't really done a damn thing that wasn't motivated by self-preservation for the past few years. And I don't apologize for that. But I also don't wear it as a badge of honor.

I've always been the smart kid. Always. I've banked on that for my entire life. Straight As, good at piano, witty, passionate, motivated. Eloquent. Compassionate.

Neurotic.

That night that I twisted your arm into "hanging out" with me... I have tried and tried to put into words how disconnected from everything I felt—myself, other people, the world, reality. Without an ounce of exaggeration, I felt like I was drowning. I never would have been so coercive if I hadn't literally felt like I was making a move to save my own life.

If you hadn't been in the right place at the right time—if you had never asked the simple, innocent question, "Is everything okay?" I never would have latched onto you like a leech. A blood-sucking, neurotic, emotionally needy, controlling, infuriating, angry leech.

I'm still working out whether any crush I had was mostly

due to the fact that you were essentially, by coincidence, the person who threw me the lifesaver when I most needed one.

Not that you're not charming; I just usually don't do crushes. Messy. The indignant feminist incubated within a literal misogynistic hellhole in me has always had a great deal of pride in her ability to be logically separatist in her emotions towards people, when it comes to any romantic capacity.

How else to avoid tripping and falling into a life-sucking, child-bearing, and most likely ultimately loveless marriage? How else to accomplish any of her own dreams or goals?

I was so awkward because I was so trapped in my head, in the internal chaos, in the past, in "remembering who I was," as I know I've put it before. Taking in new information was always a rude interruption. Rumination was compulsive and incessant.

I had been looking for someone to rescue me from my head. And you asked if I was okay. So you were the unlucky appointee to my own personal Hunger Games.

I'm glad you made it out alive.

And I was overbearing; a hurricane of post-adolescent and postponed-adolescent confusion and angst and crisis after crisis. I was overwhelming.

I am so sorry.

I never let you be a person. I never let you talk. I don't know if you wanted to. But I didn't let you.

You learned to shut up. You knew I wouldn't.

The emotions were always separate. There are at least two Kims. This is no Tumblr stretch of the imagination. This is real.

There is—and was—the me that thought things through, logically, and the me that held all the feelings. And they couldn't touch, like different food items in cordoned off sections of a dinner plate.

I'm still not sure if they touch.

And you got all of the feelings, while I was sitting there, wherever I was, usually in my room, on my bed, crouched in a corner, trying to put it all back together again.

There were so many fucking goddamn feelings; all at once, nearly all at full intensity; some I had no words for; and so I incoherently tried to put words to them, so they would settle down or go away.

But you still hadn't noticed me. That was the plan. To be noticed. To stop feeling invisible. To stop being that teenager, caught in a horrific slow lapse of time, all of hell and the weight of the world breathing down my neck, because my entire life had been a lie.

My parents had lied to me.

My teachers had lied to me.

My extended family had lied to me.

My friends had lied to me.

My pastors—my spiritual leaders—the guides and guardians of my soul from this world through the gates to the next—had.

Lied.

To.

Me.

I'm going to use this word one more time because I know how fucking sick you are hearing it from me—trauma stops time. There is, to this day, a part of me that is stuck back there, trying to deny that what was happening was happening, trying not to exist, trying to preserve what sense of self I had, but unable to do that in a way that kept me and my emotions together. So split off they went, down different pathways, for years to come.

And you got so close to noticing me.

I almost felt found.

But then you sort of ruined it by assuming I was hitting on you.

Calm down, Zac Efron.

I was much too shy to be doing that at the time.

I was also pretty busy trying to hold the entire world together in my head. Not much energy left for flirting.

I would go on to do that.

But at the time, that kind of hurt.

I was just trying to be found.

I was just trying to exist again.

I was too lost in my head to be cognizant of how awkward I looked and acted; I knew it, from memory, and from other people's reactions to me. Which always, of course, made things all the more awkward; that complete lack of self-awareness, only this time it was through no fault of mine.

I'm still sorry that it ended up dragging on for as long as it did until I realized I have to find myself. And not in a "discovering who you really are at the peak of Mount Everest or at the edge of the Pacific Ocean or in the middle of a desert" kind of way. Not the kind of finding yourself people claim to be doing in college. The "becoming who you needed when you most needed someone" kind of way. The kind of person sixteen-year-old me needed. Still needs.

It wasn't you.

You didn't deserve those expectations.

You are so great.

You have so many merits of your own that I hope you take pride in every day.

But you weren't my savior.

You weren't my God surrogate.

You threw me a line, and I latched on. But I could have kept swimming.

And I should have let go a long time ago.

I'm so sorry I ruined any chance we had at a normal

friendship years ago by placing those expectations on you. I'm still getting better. I still struggle. I still wish for death. That's not a joke. That has never been a joke. I still search inside of myself, daily, for any clue that I am still remotely the same person I was years ago. I still "come to" and realize I was feeling things in my head, and thinking with my heart. I still assume that everyone thinks I'm crazy.

I still have crazy girl hair :)

And I still have this incessant need to explain myself—to most people, but mostly, to the person who got the closest that anyone had ever gotten to finding me, just by asking the right question at the right time.

You don't need those explanations.

I do.

Sixteen-year-old me does.

Or thinks she does.

For the record, sixteen-year-old me would probably have thought you were pretty cute too.

She would have been elated you had a sense of humor.

She would have been over the moon that you cared about people.

She would have been weirded out that you wanted to talk to her at all.

(She was a weird kid.)

You deserve all the good things, Andrews. And you've worked for them. And I hope you get them. I really, really do.

Thank you.

EPILOGUE

Though this last message makes it sound as if I had finally reached some closure, the truth is I continued messaging him with "vents" for weeks after. The frequency with which I would unload on him was also much greater than what is indicated here; this is just a sample of some of the most poignant highlights from over a year's worth of introspection.

Like my friend (we'll call him Owen, and I always did call him by his last name, which we'll say for purposes of this story is Andrews, as referenced in the message above) told me once—he's not a Word doc. I would have to expect some sort of reply, even if they came very rarely.

And yeah, maybe I could have done all this reflection to myself—but no. It's the sharing that makes introspection all the more meaningful. I think most writers realize that inherently, even if they never put words to the thought itself.

I'm gradually making it to a better and better place, and will hopefully start attending therapy semi-regularly again after my therapist returns from her maternity leave next month. But I'll always be grateful for makeshift therapists in the form of flawed and busy friends who leave their inboxes open and your messages on read, for letting me feel like I had a voice and an audience, however small, right at the time in my life I needed both more than ever before.

I hope that you, reading this now, have found your voice. And if you haven't yet, my best time-worn suggestion is to pick up a pen and paper, or your nearest word processing device, and pour your heart out to a friend... Even if that friend is someone you haven't met yet. You might be surprised at what you find inside yourself.

STAGE IV

Depression

"I desire the things which will destroy me in the end."

—SYLVIA PLATH

THE HARD TRUTH

SARAH MAE EKHOLM

*The hard truth catches in my throat and suffocates
    me*
*until retching I spit it out in one heaving, writhing
    ball.*
It's an embryonic mass, quivering in my shaky gaze
*with a heart of cold granite, smooth and
    impenetrable.*
*It slips from my desperate fingers to roll away, sodden
    and slick.*
It drifts, wandering through the space between us.

LET PEOPLE FEEL

MARISSA ALEXA MCCOOL

Whether it's Chester Bennington, Robin Williams, Chris Cornell, or any other person in the mainstream awareness that passes away from these circumstances, the same responses are always so irritatingly prevalent.

"You didn't know them. Stop pretending like you did."

"Suicide is the coward's way out."

"He abandoned his family."

"Permanent solution to a temporary problem."

"Fuck them, I didn't like their work anyway."

I'm curious why it is so many people seem determined to remove the agency of how people feel from the conversation. What is it about feelings, especially surrounding one of the most difficult situations a person can deal with, that causes others to speak up about how others shouldn't feel a certain way?

As I described in the last chapter, I recently went through the loss of a friend of fourteen years, the eighteenth person I've known in my life to have left via suicide. This was shortly before Chester Bennington of Linkin Park resurrected the same conversation I hear as mentioned above, so my feelings are still sort of raw on the topic, and I've had to avoid a lot of threads based on that.

What I can't understand is how some people seem determined to not let anyone feel or grieve, whether it's because they didn't care about the person's work, or because they're unwilling to acknowledge the impact artists can have on our lives.

I had this conversation a lot when Robin Williams passed, and the graphics and memes were passed around where people were mourning. Whether it was because of the Genie, *Good Will Hunting*, his standup, or any of his other endeavors, he touched a lot of lives. And there was, as mentioned, the usual off-putting responses of, "He took the easy way out," "You didn't know him. Why do you care?" etc.

I think you have to wrap yourself in a layer of ignorance to not think that artists can impact our daily lives. You've seen pictures of my library. You've heard my interviews with podcasters and activists. Some I consider friends at this point, but they all started out as people who influenced me, or whose voices were prevalent in my life. Losing one of them would be devastating, because their voice or words were a part of me, even if it wasn't an interpersonal connection.

For many of us who grew up in the late 90s, Linkin Park's *Hybrid Theory* managed to capture an essence of rebellious youth, of suffering, of being angry and not necessarily knowing why. It was my entire freshman year, especially being in and out of the hospital.

Granted, I moved on from it rather quickly, especially when an album of remixes came out. It didn't catch me anymore, but for that brief moment in time, that screaming and raw emotion captured my inner conflict of the time.

That level of angst was so real for many of us, especially post-9/11 when those of us who were social outcasts were singled out and pushed away. I didn't last an entire school year after that happened, partially because I wasn't interested in conforming to my elitist school's image of what a student should be.

Many of us were pushed out the same way. That's part of what *Voice in the Dark* was really trying to recapture; a time in my life where it seemed like the management was more interested in pushing us away for not wanting to fit a certain model of a student or citizen.

But sometimes, someone who speaks up about those things the most ends up losing their battle with mental illness. Then people call them a coward or someone who abandoned their family or a quitter or a piece of shit for leaving people behind, and you stand there and wonder, "Gee, I can't imagine why people don't speak up about these feelings when they have them."

When you stigmatize mental illness, or refer to anyone on anti-depressants as weak, crazy, or say that they just need to go outside, the world can feel empty and alone. People don't want to reach out for help because they don't want to be belittled, insulted, or condescended to. Or even worse, proselytized.

I sat through the funeral for a friend recently, and I saw little to no reflection of who my friend was. Instead I heard about Jesus and heaven and the same stories we've always heard, but I went there to remember my friend. I cannot emphasize that enough. I kept my mouth shut, even though I know when I'm being stared at (it was a Catholic service), but this was like Aiden's grandmother's service. Thirty seconds on his grandmother, twenty-nine minutes and thirty seconds on Jesus and the Rapture and going to heaven and salvation.

Maybe it's because I was raised in a family where you talked about and celebrated the person when they passed, but this seems so foreign to me. I didn't get that experience of remembering the person until a bunch of us who were friends back in the day sat around a table at the diner and reminisced, laughed, and even teased. To me, that's always been how to remember someone, and I wish more of that was incorporated into remembrances such as that.

I'd rather remember my friend who was an amazing musician than what Jesus said about X. I'd rather acknowledge that he thought he was way better at martial arts than he was, which led to him getting dumped on his ass a few times, than hear about how God called him home because X. It seems so fake, and more to convince people that they shouldn't be sad because they lost someone because better tomorrow or something.

I mean no disrespect to anyone for whom that is a comfort, but distracting from what's going on, in my experience, has never been a healthy method of coping. Remembering who the person was and what they meant to you? That's how you learn to accept what has happened, and remember them fondly.

Yet we don't allow people to feel this way when it comes to the death of an artist or celebrity, because you didn't meet them or know them, so that means you're not allowed to feel. Feelings are constantly invalidated by those others who are uncomfortable with them, because god forbid things are being discussed that don't involve you, or are about someone you didn't personally admire.

Whether it's about the death of a celebrity, our experience as LGBT people, or anything else that anyone has to deal with, there's always someone out to tell us what is more important that we're not focusing on, what is more important than whatever it is being discussed. "Why do you care about X when Y is happening and nobody's talking about it?"

And usually, whichever Y is, they don't do anything about

it. They only want to stop the conversation, pat themselves on the back for pretending to care about an issue, and then move on like nothing happened because conversation about feelings outside of their box made them uncomfortable, and we can't be having that shit going on.

Feel what you feel. If an artist meant something to you, celebrate their presence in your life. If a writer captures your imagination, you're under no obligation to pretend that meant nothing to you when they pass. And for the love of everything, don't invalidate how someone feels upon their passing just because it isn't how you feel. We have to deal with that enough without adding grief to something that can't be expressed without being explained to why it's wrong and being constantly invalidated.

HANG ON TIGHTER

NATHAN DICKEY

TW: Discussion of depression and suicide.

During a Friday night of drinking in the summer of 2012, I found myself lying on concrete outside—where I had fallen on my way toward the nearby freeway overpass—and sobbing intensely. The rest of that night is a blur to me now, but some details remain clear.

Finding myself in the hospital. Being escorted down a brightly lit corridor and into a small room to be questioned by a mental health practitioner. Being monitored until morning, when I was told to do my best to find a support system, then finally released and taken back to the university campus where I lived at the time.

I was a twenty-five-year-old journalism student minoring in philosophy when I decided to take my own life. I don't recall a specific trigger. Something just came to a head. The depression I struggled with my whole life, and about which I had kept mostly silent, became unbearably oppressive that evening, and I felt more alone than I had ever felt before.

Depression had always hung over me like a dark cloud for

most of my life. I grew up in a fundamentalist religious environment that viewed depression as a moral failing, and so it was not until I broke away from religion that I recognized my own depression as the medical condition it is.

From the time I was a teenager, I had built a wall between myself and other people because I always felt somehow different from everyone I knew. It wasn't until much later that I learned I suffered from Asperger syndrome, but I recognized my social awkwardness and difficulty in parsing social cues and engaging in "small talk." People have told me they don't speak my language, that I'm eccentric and that if I fit in anywhere, it would always be as the "token single sidekick guy."

And so it was that, after graduating high school, I embraced the solitary life at first. When I was in the process of doubting and breaking away from the religious worldview I was raised in, my internal monologue went something like this: "I just can't relate to anybody. Fuck it, I'll do life by myself! I have my books, my music, and all these new ideas I'm exploring. Life of the mind FTW!"

And yet much of my free time on weekend nights was spent observing people while driving and walking the streets of downtown Boise by myself. I studied the way friends and lovers interacted. I identified so closely with the character Travis Bickle from the movie *Taxi Driver* that I started interpreting it as a cautionary tale about how pathological loneliness could change a person in a very bad way.

A few years later, I was in college and no longer wanted to be alone. I decided to tear that wall down by trying to understand other people. I tried to resurrect that five-year-old child who would walk around with a notebook and pen in public and at social gatherings, asking children and adults questions about their lives and recording their answers.

I took up journalism in college, directing my attention

away from myself and towards other people and events external to me. My newfound interest in skepticism led me to examine the various ways in which modern media, particularly television news, distorted facts and the publics' perception of those facts. I aspired to become an investigative journalist in the muckraking tradition.

But I was neglecting self-care and shoving the depression I knew I carried with me under a rug. I started becoming a stranger to myself. And I nearly lost myself permanently that dark summer night.

At the time of this writing, five years have passed since that night. I still look back on it as the event that catalyzed my will to hang onto life for as long as I can. I had to almost die to understand that I have it within me to take the first step of assigning value to living and then to take the next thousand steps of contributing to the wellbeing of other people.

After that night, I was not *just* someone who had let go of the concept of god and religion. I was not *just* the man in the Stephen Crane poem who told the universe, "Sir, I exist," only to hear the universe respond, "The fact has not created in me a sense of obligation." I *also* found the courage to reach out and grabbed hold of humanism and the friendships I have been fortunate to cultivate.

My depression is still with me. I am still dangling from a precipice, hanging over an abyss. But the important thing is that I am still hanging on, thanks in no small part to a combination of antidepressant medication and one-on-one therapy with a mental health counselor. My hands are no longer bloody from grasping bare, cold rock. I'm holding on to the helping hands of my fellow human beings, who are in turn holding on to others.

As I write these words, I'm listening to a silly but sweet pop song from the 70s called *Tighter, Tighter* by a one-hit wonder called Alive N Kickin' that encourages its listeners to "hold on just a little bit tighter now." You may laugh, but I have no shame in that song being part of my life soundtrack.

The thing is, we are *all* hanging over the abyss. This is the human condition. A very good friend of mine, who has been kind enough to check in on my mental health from time to time, stated the case very beautifully when she wrote this to me during a late-night IM chat: "It's so true that to be human is to be vulnerable, exposed. Susceptible. Fragile. Control is an illusion. We are so small, and yet have such capacity for suffering and for joy. And yet it's all so... perilous. I think to be human is to be in peril."

Many of us are just hanging lower in the darkness than the rest on the chain and farther away from the light at the top. That light is not some platonically pure, ideal heaven that religion wrongly tells us exists. No, the philosopher (or new wave pop singer, if you prefer) Belinda Carlisle had the right idea when she sang, "Heaven is a place on Earth." All we have is each other to make life in this cold, indifferent, and inhospitable universe just a little more warm and bearable.

Embrace that warmth while you can. Each one of us, every single human being alive at this moment, is eventually going to lose their grip and fall into the abyss. There is nothing any of us can do to change that cold, hard individual condition, no matter how hard we rage against the dying of light.

But there's more to the human condition than that tragic individual part. There is the *social* part, which is what keeps me (and most other people) going.

Yes, that social condition is often fucking tragic as well. But it does not *have* to be. We have art, music, sex, books, and humor. We can fight for social justice, be an ally to marginalized, misunderstood, and oppressed minorities and identities. We can stand up for a rational, scientific, and empathetic understanding of the world, and in so doing hit upon ever-improving agricultural technologies to feed the starving masses.

We can apply the knowledge of how the purposeless and unguided paths of evolution work in order to create our own purpose and direction in the form of vaccines that eradicate disease completely. We can galvanize against complacency and short-term gratification to mitigate climate disruption and save the planet from becoming an oven.

This is why we rage against the dying of the light.

To everyone reading this who, like myself, currently suffers from depression or any number of other mental condition, I want to say this: You. Are. Not. Crazy. You are not an aberration. I know firsthand what it's like to shout and scream and feel like nobody can hear you. I have felt and continue to feel that way many times. But you are never as alone as you feel. If nothing else, you can reach out to me.

I am thirty years old now, at the time of this writing. Thirty is a scary number, because it's the age at which, according to largely-unspoken social expectations, you're supposed to have figured out who you are and settled on what you're going to do for the remainder of your life.

But luckily for me and most other people around my age, life is not a game of *Logan's Run*. I'm still not entirely sure who I am or what I want to do, career-wise.

In fact, I sometimes feel like a complete stranger to myself, and it sometimes feels as if staying alive is a matter of learning to trust this person I don't know.

My current therapist tells me this feeling is a classic symptom of depression. What I do know is that I'm a survivor. I do know that I value the lives of the people I have not even met in person yet who have given me their friendship. I do know that I'm extremely grateful to have been given a voice, however small, in the skeptical and secular humanist podcasting community through my podcast *Trolling with Logic*, where I have not only had the opportunity to apply the interviewing skills I learned in college toward interacting with many wonderful and fascinating people, but where I also have a platform from which to advocate for other people who are far less privileged than I.

And knowing all that as a starting point is enough for now.

Lovingly dedicated to the memory of television news reporter Christine Chubbuck (1944 – 1974).

LOSS

AIDEN XAVIER MCCOOL

The year 1998 stubbornly sticks out in my memory. I'm certain that no matter how much time passes it will always haunt me like a faded, deformed scar that will never quite go away; and if I press hard enough on that scar, I find myself back there again.

I changed that year, and even now I am still somewhat bitter and resentful over it; I liked exactly who I was back then, and I didn't want to change one little bit. It seems that I had no other choice than to go along with it in order to survive; since there is no feasible way for one to go back, I felt like I lost myself and I have yet to recover from that.

It was August, and we were going on our annual summer vacation up to Groton, CT to visit my uncle. This was an event I looked forward to every year. My uncle lived alone at the time, and he and I were extremely close.

As he was still enlisted in the Navy, he always found a way to take us on a tour of a few Submarines, or a Battle Cruiser or two; there was always time for at least one night at the local race track too. This year, my older cousin was invited along with us; although I was excited, something felt off and I couldn't shake it.

The afternoon we left was such a beautiful day. The sky was a deep blue, and not a single cloud was present. I was so excited as I ran around our front yard, watching Mom and Dad load up the car. Grandma was there with my younger cousin—who was too young to go on the trip—to see us off before we left.

I had an odd sense of dread that I couldn't quite explain. As I looked out the window at the two of them, I couldn't help but think, "Stay here, you'll be much safer that way." I disregarded that thought quickly, as I was only five and didn't like that thought at all; so instead I focused on getting on the road and how much fun we'd have later on.

The majority of the trip went as expected: We saw a few submarines and other ships owned by the Navy, we went to the local mall, and to the local race track—where dad got to live out one of his dreams and assist one of the pit crews during the race. But there was one item added to that year's itinerary that hadn't been there before.

Mom expressed interest in going to see the mansions in Newport, RI—which was a few hours' drive. It seemed like a bad idea, though, as it was overcast and rainy outside; we weren't sure if any of the mansions would Mom and Dad talked it over, and he put it to a vote. When all of us expressed interest in going, it was settled.

After breakfast, all six of us loaded up into our purple Dodge Stratus. I had that sense of dread once again. Before getting in. I remember thinking, "I hope we don't get into an accident today." Once again, being so young, I was able to put that thought to the back of my mind as I was buckled in on the passenger's side of the car.

To this day, I can't confirm if I actually fell asleep, or if I've willingly blocked out the rest of that car ride. I can say with certainty that the next thing I consciously remember is hearing sirens and my body shaking. I know now that I was riding in the back of an ambulance. I didn't know why, at least not yet. I was content to believe that I was dreaming at that point.

It ceased being a dream when the ambulance came to a stop, and I heard so many voices all around me. When I thought no one was looking, I became brave enough to open my eyes and take a look around. Tan walls, three windows to my right, and a doctor on my left, right by my head. I wasn't in the car anymore.

I didn't know what was going on. I panicked and tried to pretend I was asleep, thinking that I would be left alone if they thought I was sleeping. I was given a sedative in each arm, and I hated myself for mouthing, "Ow!" I thought I was going to be in big trouble after that.

The next thing I knew, I was in a hospital bed, and my uncle was in a similar bed to my left. He barely had a scratch on him, but he looked terrible. It wouldn't be until after successive visits from my aunts, uncles, and grandparents that I found out my fears were confirmed.

We had been in a car accident. I had been told that my mother, brother, and cousin were all in a separate hospital recovering. I assumed Dad had to be there too, despite the fact that no one said anything about his location or condition.

I'm not sure if it was out of respect, or out of sympathy that they waited to tell me that he died. I wouldn't hear about it until I saw Mom in the hospital a few days later.

Some people believe that children do not understand the concept of death when that is the furthest thing from the truth. The world as I knew it shattered, one of the people I knew I could depend on always had vanished forever, and my sense of security had suddenly been challenged.

I worried for months that one day Mom would be gone too; there were years where I wouldn't sleep because I thought the same would happen to me. Even as adults, we have a hard time accepting our mortality; it's an extremely heavy burden for children to accept at such a young age.

I clung for a few days to the hope that there had been a mistake, that he had been sent to another hospital or had been left behind, and therefore had a longer recovery time. I didn't stop believing that until the day they took the stitches from my forehead out. I knew that whenever I was in pain, or scared, or sad, I could call out for dad; and although he couldn't always make it stop, he could make me feel better.

The removal was painful. In their rush to stabilize me, the hospital had sewn the short hairs on my scalp into the stitches. I screamed, I cried, and it wouldn't stop. My grandmother tried her very best to comfort me, but it wasn't the same; the pain was too much, and Dad wasn't there to make things a little better.

I looked at Grandma, hoping my last plea would bring forth some miracle. "I want my Daddy" I sobbed. It broke her heart, and he still didn't come back. I wouldn't be forced to face this fact until I saw a mock casket at his funeral a few weeks later. It was all the proof that I need to realize that there had been no mistake—he was gone for good.

Everything changed after that. It was hard to be happy and carefree about life. I knew that I was not going to live forever; anything could happen at any time, and I was no longer as obliviously fearless as I had been before we left on that trip.

It's had its pros as well as its cons. I became aware of my mortality much earlier than most people do, which made me conscious about some of my decisions. Yet it made me jaded about my youth and put me at odds with a lot of my peers growing up, not being able to feel immortal, or forever young.

I often feel that this forced me to grow up much faster than I should've. I don't feel as if I had enough time to enjoy my childhood to the fullest before feeling the rough hand of reality strike me down.

I've found that it's pointless to direct my anger, since no one involved was entirely at fault. Terrible things happen without reason all the time. It's impossible to turn back time, or regain the time I've lost.

So, what to do with the bitterness, the anger, and the grief that still hang suspended? The truth is that I haven't figured that out yet, and I doubt that I will anytime soon. I hope that I can have that resolution before I die, not in order to finally put it behind me; but to prevent it from hurting me anymore.

COPING WITH LOSS
MARISSA ALEXA MCCOOL

For those of you who have followed me long enough to have heard *Inciting Incident #30*, pre-transition and all, you'll know that I've had a long history with suicide in my life. I wrote a movie about it in 2015, and that was the first of many times I'd use the song *I Believe*.

Eighteen. Eighteen people. That's how many I've known since the first time I lost an acquaintance that way in ninth grade. An ex-neighbor, a co-worker, a friend, a tag team partner, an ex-girlfriend, and so many others make up the rest of that list.

However, this one was probably the toughest one I've ever had to deal with; not just because it was someone I'd known for fourteen years, not just because of the family he left behind, but because thinking about it made me realize how much of an influence this guy had on my life.

Brian and I went back to 2003, when I first started hanging out with new people again. At that point in my life, I'd made the mistake of returning from Florida so soon because I was homesick. Or rather, friendsick. What else could you expect from someone who was supposed to be in their junior year of high school, but had graduated instead?

Brian was one of many I met at another Brian's birthday party. The other Brian had been my friend since sixth grade and went through junior high with me. However, he'd gone to the Catholic high school in our area as opposed to mine, and therefore had found a completely new circle of friends. With me having returned, he brought me into that circle, which included this Brian.

He and I became close a few months later, when I went to the junior prom with them, and attended the YMCA lock-in afterward. I remember well how he and I sat against a wall talking while his date slept on him. He was the first of many friends with whom I had a lot in common personality-wise, but were extremely different in philosophy and life experience. It made for interesting conversations, disagreements, and even fallings out at several points in our lives.

As I've been slowly remembering different ways he was involved in my life, I've been struggling with tensions in many places. He introduced me to my favorite band, among many others, could do a dead-on Denis Leary impression, shared many sleepovers and events, was in my first wedding, and also capitulated my first serious relationship ending.

That's been my biggest point of struggle—remembering that things were far from copacetic over the years we knew each other. We mended fences a few years ago, and I'm grateful for that especially now, but I've been feeling guilty for the fact that at two distinct points in my life, he did a terrible thing to me. I don't need to go into what they were, because that's not the point of this essay, but I've been fighting the guilt demon for also thinking about those points in our time together.

At funerals and times of remembrance, you're supposed to

talk about the good things and reflect on the person fondly, right? Especially under these circumstances, with leaving a little girl behind and a grieving family, isn't it a disservice to remember that he also betrayed your trust?

It's also true though that those friendships that go through some struggle and issues are the ones that become stronger in the end. Did that happen with ours? Possibly. I can't say for sure, but I do know we came to a new point of understanding before our friendship met its untimely end last week.

My relationship with this friend was tumultuous longer than it was stable. We were co-workers, roommates, and close friends, but at points, we were also in arguments, disagreements, betrayals, blow-ups, and periods of silence.

That's life, though. More relationships you have will have unpleasant parts than not. But it doesn't resolve the feeling of guilt when remembering those times when they pass away, especially in such a manner and under such circumstances. Intellectually, you know there's nothing you could've done. Logically, you know there's nothing you could've done.

But then you remember that the last time you saw each other, you promised to catch up. You remember that you could've reached out at a couple points, and somehow missed each other. You find out that there was a lot going on that you missed because of your travel schedule and other engagements, and feel like the worst friend on the planet for having no idea of what was transpiring.

Such is the untimely loss of a friend.

Tonight, I'll be attending his viewing. There's a lot of religiosity and conservatism in this family, and the funeral tomorrow will be a full Catholic service. Those things would make me uncomfortable before I transitioned, but right now, with the way things are and the atmosphere in which we live, you'll have to forgive me if I'm not somewhat uneasy knowing how I might be received since almost no one attending this service will have seen me since I started transitioning.

It's not about me, and I'm not going for them. The same as I know I couldn't have changed the outcome, even if he had reached out. But that doesn't change the guilt I feel, the heartbreak I'm experiencing, and the fear of facing those that either didn't know or don't agree with it. I don't feel that's unreasonable. It's acknowledging that while good things may take place, and there will certainly be those, potentially bad things may also occur. It's not pessimistic; rather, it's realistic to consider both sides of the equation.

Just the same as you have to do with a friendship when it comes to an end in such fashion. It's not unfair to the person who passed if you remember the bad times along with the good, because that's how they're a person. To gloss over that is to disregard part of your story together. Just because it's come to an end doesn't mean you tear that chapter out of the book.

That being said, it's going to be hard to read through that chapter when you pick up that book again, no matter how much you know that it doesn't make you a bad person for doing so. The only thing you can really do is make the best of the situation, and try to be there for those who are hurting worse than you are.

But this one hurts. Badly. Damn, man. I wish I knew you were feeling such pain.

Rest in peace, Brian Michael Johns.

STAGE V

Acceptance

"There is no exquisite beauty ... without some strangeness in the proportion."

—EDGAR ALLAN POE

NAME DAY

MARISSA ALEXA MCCOOL

I was eighteen years old. I had long, dark hair and weighed maybe 150 pounds soaking wet. At the time, I wasn't entirely closed off to the idea that I was different, but I thought it was more of a "goth" thing than anything else.

Most of my friends were girls, I related to girls, I preferred hanging out with girls, but I hadn't yet put the pieces together. I still wouldn't entirely, but this point in my life was where everything changed forever. It was the time I got the name Marissa, and it stuck.

My friend Teresa had an ex-boyfriend who wouldn't leave her alone. She tried saying that she had a new boyfriend, but the guy wouldn't take that as a reason to stop bothering her. I was there after one of these phone conversations, and she got what was seemingly the most random idea ever: "What if I pretended to have a girlfriend?"

Sure, why not? It was better to come up with solutions like that rather than worry about real-life things like harassment or stalking.

I supported the idea, going along with it as it would make

one of my friends happy to get rid of this guy that was clearly toxic to her physical and mental health.

"Wouldn't take 'no' for an answer" is a gross understatement.

The guy's response is what triggered the whole event. He said that he wanted to meet this girl, as if he had to check her over for proof and approval or something. Teresa was not exactly a social butterfly, so this posed a problem: How would she get a girl to not only pretend to be her girlfriend, but go along with this? Go out on a "date" with her to meet the guy and show him once and for all that she had moved on?

Teresa turned to me and asked, "Would you pretend to be my girlfriend Marissa?"

I don't know why she picked that name. I don't know why she thought of having me dress up rather than asking an AFAB person she knew. I have no idea why any of that seemed a reasonable solution to this problem, but it was what she came up with. I didn't even hesitate, for reasons that I reflectively saw as an opportunity, and agreed nearly instantaneously.

The first part was taking me out to get some appropriate clothing. I'd done makeup and "joke" dress-ups before, but never something designed to "pass" enough for another guy to acknowledge.

I know for a fact that our choices weren't that good, because it was my only outfit for when this continued, and when we took it to a gay friend (who later came out as trans herself), it got the "Oh, honey ..." treatment.

It was a long black skirt, white shirt, and denim-style shawl. It would be years before I'd understand anything even resembling fashion sense. That day was not this day, but it served its purpose.

Several other of her friends got in on this idea, and it was going to be a group of four of us going on this date to the café, which I would later work in for a while, and we'd be meeting this guy there so that he could meet Marissa.

Teresa asked what my last name would be. My girlfriend at the time, Kaylene, had the last name McCool, and I always thought that was the best last name ever, and I'm also a stickler for alliteration. Therefore, I went with Marissa McCool, because it sounded awesome.

I had no idea how long that would stick with me, even through Kaylene and I going through patches of not speaking to each other, sometimes for years, before resolving things.

Another one of her friends did my makeup. Kept it subtle —light browns, contouring, the whole nine yards. I'd never had much body hair, and I had started shaving my legs in tenth grade anyway. My skin was soft, my hair was long, I was skinny as a rail, and I could pull off a falsetto pretty easily. I was feeling so many different kinds of things while getting prepared for this that I reflectively realize was my true self-awakening.

The false presentation I made as a public persona was enthusiastic, outgoing, loud, and flirtatious. Once I was Marissa, I was demure, quiet, shy, a bit giggly, and cautious. It was seemingly the exact opposite of who people thought I was at the time.

Getting in the car and having everyone address me with female pronouns and a new name was absolutely invigorating. Butterflies rose, and a tingling in my heart that I'd never noticed before made itself known. This was right. I had no fear about being "caught" or otherwise in danger, because I was with three other people. It was before I was completely socially aware of homophobia, let alone transphobia, especially because I didn't even know trans was a thing at the time.

The meeting at the café went absolutely brilliantly, and Teresa even kissed me to top the whole thing off. The café crowd stared at us when we did it, but who cares? It was amazing. I took pictures with everyone who went along with me, pictures I wouldn't end up losing until years later through other traumatic events.

The high that I got from being out in public as Marissa was addicting. It wouldn't be long after that that I'd dress up at Otakon and spend the entire night addicted to the feeling I would get as people would look at me and talk to me as Marissa. I couldn't put my finger on it at the time, but not only was the way they spoke to me different, but how I felt speaking to other people was. Different isn't even the word; in hindsight, it was more authentic.

We all have presentations that we put on when we're expected to act a certain way, whether it be for family, religion, school, or any other social setting. For some people, it doesn't change; they're always who they are. For those of us who were raised to feel that introverted was a bad thing and we needed to be outgoing in order to be successful and liked, we developed a presentation persona that tried to fit the attributes of the approved social dynamic. I didn't realize I'd been putting one on until these times at eighteen.

Not only did I go to a convention dressed up, but a few of my friends would tell me to get dressed up so we could go to stores late at night together, just to see the looks we'd get. I pretended to think it was funny at the time, just because it was better to feel like they were laughing with me, rather than the looks I knew I'd get if I wanted to do this more often or for more than a joke.

It was indirect approval, but it was approval nonetheless. I liked who I was when I was Marissa, and I wanted that feeling to continue as much as possible. I only wish I'd known what resources and words were out there, because with the right place and time, maybe I would've started transitioning years ago and avoided nights of fear, crying, and reasons I'd give myself that I couldn't end up living as who I am.

I don't have the data for how much information like that being more accessible to young kids has saved their lives, even with the rampant social transphobia that continues to this day, but I do know that my life would've been forever changed and improved had I had it, and I might've avoided years of unsuccessful and heart-breaking relationships that were mostly due to my complete inability to be what I thought I needed to be, who they thought they were getting into a relationship with, and what society expected of someone who appeared to be of my stature.

COMING OUT

TIM BROWN

I t took me forty-two years to be me.

I was born in rural Mississippi, not that there is anything besides rural in Mississippi. I only lived there for nine days. But it was long enough to count, unfortunately.

I joke with my mom that she should could have pulled her shit together long enough to get in the car and drive into Alabama to birth me. It might only be one rung up the progressive ladder, but that one rung makes a difference.

I was born into the family of a Southern Baptist pastor. My dad and mom had moved to Mississippi to attend Clarke College, a Baptist school. This conservative, evangelical world became the context to my life. There were both good and bad that come with such a context. I have chosen to focus on the good.

I loved living in the rural parts of Alabama as a teenager. We lived near a large lake, and later built a house on the lakefront. I swam, skied, boated, and road other watercraft almost all summer long.

It was a beautiful place. I was always around people. We had a very social family and church circle. And, I was the center of attention whenever the situation allowed. When the situation didn't allow for it, I found a way to make it happen. I was a mischievous child, constantly into everything. I never did shut up. There was a reason why.

I was a skinny kid, and I was struggling with my identity in an environment that didn't allow for questioning such things. I didn't know enough to say that I had a sexual identity crisis. These words were not in the working vocabulary of a rural, evangelical Christian, conservative town.

In the absence of understanding how to express myself, I defaulted to the only thing to take away attention from it. I talked constantly. I joked incessantly. I would take command of conversations and rooms so that my presence was known. I would use self-deprecating humor to beat people to the punch.

All of this made me the funny and popular kid that I was. I believe that this was already a part of my genetic makeup. But I certainly honed the skills. So I did enjoy life, school, church, and all the other social settings of a childhood. I made the most of them.

Looking back, I realize how important it is to have loving and caring parents. While my parents are still conservative and don't agree with me on everything, they never interfere.

I've watched them love people all my life. They loved everybody. They loved poor people, white people, black, brown, gay, straight ... everybody. They loved people who hurt them. They loved people who took advantage of them. It was an amazing thing to experience.

They loved people well. They loved me well. They still do. And I think they always knew that I was different.

I tried so hard to be the jock my dad was. He was the consummate and decorated athlete. He was a star football player. He could, and did, play every sport. He did so very well. I played them all too. And I did so very poorly.

I sucked. I was pretty fast, but that was the extent of it.

In our little world, there was football, baseball, and basketball. Everything else was from the devil—not really, but if you didn't play one of those, you were a sissy. We couldn't even spell "soccer" back then.

I have heard people say that practice makes perfect. Betch, please. I practiced as much as everyone else. I still sucked.

There were many times I can recall my parents putting their own interests aside for me and my sister, but one in particular sticks out. I had to play a basketball game. My dad took me to the game. Now remember, this is the guy who was well-known for his athletic prowess. To this day, people stop him and ask him about plays he made, some which hold records.

This same man sat at my game while I rode the bench. He did in every time. But I remember this particular time I didn't play at all. On the way home, he was encouraging me. He never criticized me.

When we got home, he set up an obstacle course around which I could dribble the ball. He coached me. He didn't pick out my mistakes. He gently corrected me. When I did something right, which was infrequent, he cheered and celebrated.

My mom was similar. She was, and is, the most understated person I know. She is a pillar of quiet strength. She sacrificed everything to put us and others first. She cooked, cleaned, and worked some outside the home. Mostly she maintained our house with near perfection. At one period in high school, she was substitute teaching. She was loved by the students and the staff. So she got a lot of opportunities.

One day, I was planning to skip school the following day.

That night before, I was in the living room with my mom and some people who had come to visit. She mentioned that she might fill in for a teacher the next day. In fear that that would mess up my plans for skipping, I blurted out, "You can't." She asked why. I quickly and stupidly responded, "It's embarrassing."

I was immediately devastated that I was so concerned about my plans that I hurt her. She didn't say a word.

I wanted to say all of this so that people understand the context of my coming out. My parents, my church friends, the adults in my community—these were wonderful people. But we were all taught to believe things. Some of those things were good, but some of them hurt others and still do.

I felt loved and cared for by so many people. I wouldn't take anything for that. There was just one thing that I could not do, and it took me years, many years to get to a place where I could.

As long as I perpetuated the same beliefs about homosexuality, I would be accepted in my community. So that is what I did. It was ingrained in me.

I didn't even think that I was gay. I fought it with everything I had in me. I didn't want to be gay. I was fearful that someone would find out that I had those thoughts. So I built my entire presentation on being this crazy, funny, and hard-working kid, teenager, and man.

I continued this throughout my life. I don't like to say that I created an alter ego because, then, people come back and say that I wasn't genuine. I actually was genuine. I say that an alternate persona developed as a form of defense in order to help me survive in the environment in which I had to live and survive. It was the only part of me that I could not share. And I wouldn't have early on because I didn't admit it to myself for a very long time.

I lived this struggle for the majority of my life. I dated

girls. I even truly cared about a couple of them, felt like I even loved them, but my attraction and connection was with guys.

There were a few things that kept me from coming out—actually, many, but I can list a few.

One, I simply lived in a place where there was no support. I lived in an all-white, overwhelmingly conservative, evangelical, rural community. I can't think of any way I would have been able to be out.

Two, I thought I would go to hell. You can do a lot of things in the church world, but gay isn't one of them. If you do that one, you'll be on a non-stop path to the hottest part of hell. So I just didn't entertain that this was something I could be. I felt like something was wrong with me.

There was no one around me with a counter argument to what I was taught. I felt like I had to fight and pray my way through it.

Three, I would have been isolated and ostracized. We had a gay guy come transfer to our high school. He was a cheerleader. I don't know what he was thinking, but he did not do well there.

I watched him. I realized this wasn't a possibility for anyone if they wanted to survive.

He left shortly after he got there.

Four, as I said, I didn't admit that I was gay. I was convinced this was just temptation. I would be able to fight it away.

After many years of church life, working in churches and ministry positions, the struggle only grew more difficult.

In 2008, I became a chaplain in the Army. I moved around several times and was deployed a couple. One of the moves was to Las Cruces, NM. It was there that I would begin my journey to come out.

In Las Cruces, I joined a running club in my community. I

loved it. I fell in love with running. I had to run in the Army, but now I'd finally found a way to enjoy it. Of course, that involved wonderful people and sharing some drinks now and then.

A young man showed up in our running club. He and I hit it off. I knew he was gay, but no one knew that I was. Well, they knew, probably, but I didn't admit to it.

My sister, my niece, and my cousin's son had flown back with me from Alabama to spend some time with me that summer. I invited this guy to have dinner at my house with us. My family all went to bed. He and I stayed up.

He was in my kitchen getting something from the refrigerator. I walked by and patted him on his really cute butt as I passed by. That indicated to him something was up. We ended up on the couch with some wine. He got up, came over, and kissed me. It was amazing.

We dated for about a year following that. It wasn't out in the open, but my world changed.

I eventually moved from New Mexico to North Carolina to be a chaplain with special operations at Fort Bragg. It was there that I began to be a bit more open. The problem with that is that some in the gay community are messy. Someone who was supposed to be my friend outed me at work in a horrible way. That devastated me, but it led me to own it and live it.

I had to change my endorsement. Chaplains must have the endorsement of a church denomination. Mine was Southern Baptist at the time. You can imagine that this news went over like a lead balloon.

About six months after being outed, I was sitting in my pity. I remember thinking, "I have to get out and live."

That is exactly what I did. I blew the door off the hinges. I married the guy that I had been dating. I started my own nonprofit, GOaL (Get Out and Live), and I began to speak openly about being a gay chaplain. I had opportunities availed to me to share this story on podcasts and in other ways. I even preached at a couple of churches who were affirming and supportive.

For the first time ever, I was me. I was living authentically. I never thought it was possible. I eventually started my own podcast show, *Chappy's Musings*. I don't hold back.

I had settled for forty-two years. I decided that life wasn't to be enjoyed. I figured I would spend my life making others happy. Then I realized that I could do both.

Giving to others and making sacrifices for them doesn't always mean that you have to put yourself last. Life is to be enjoyed. I hate that it took me so long to figure that out, but I don't regret it. My struggles made me tough. They are a part of my life's mosaic.

Everyone has ugly and pretty pieces in their mosaic. We don't want the ugly pieces when we are in the middle of living them out, but they shape us and mold us. One day, we can look back at the full portrait. It is then that we will see the purpose in the pain.

I am Tim. I am gay. I own my struggles.

I embrace them.

MY LOVE... THE ONE I MARRIED,
ANYWAY

MARISSA ALEXA MCCOOL

I make no secret of the fact that my husband and I are both polyamorous. If you think that's had some impact on our relationship or passion for each other, though, you haven't been around us at all.

As I sit right next to him writing this on the day that five years ago, we happened upon meeting each other, it's hard to believe we've come this far in a relatively short amount of time. I've written and been very vocal about our relationship, marriage, and how much he means to me, and while I told the story of our wedding itself in *The PC Lie*, the story of how we met is quite the event itself.

In October of 2012, my sister was getting married. Not my blood sister, but someone I'd called a sister for a good portion of my life. The joke was that we were separated at birth, something her birthmother would later claim she had no memory of, but we were as close as siblings would be, and her family treated me as such.

Our group were among the only people traveling to North

Carolina for her wedding, and since I wasn't out yet, that wasn't nearly as dangerous of an objective as it would be now.

Details about my date that evening aside, we were wandering back to our room to catch part of the Ohio State game when her grandmother pulled me aside. I suppose for clarity's sake, I should specify that Becky was adopted, but her birthmother went on to have two more kids. Her birth grandmother was the one who recognized me from Facebook, where I'd often be the big sister to Becky and jokingly tell her husband why not to say certain things. In retrospect, there were a lot of behaviors in place that were very indicative of my true self, even if I didn't connect the dots at the time.

Standing next to her grandmother was this cute, adorable person who I would later come to know as Aiden. It was only in passing, but we connected on Facebook under his deadname, and didn't really say much until a year later. For my YouTube show at the time, we were filming a game of Cards Against Humanity and were looking to get several different personalities to join us for the event.

Our conversation on Facebook began about our mutual love for the Nostalgia Critic, but ended up being an invite to come join us. My partner at the time, the same one who went to the wedding with me, fell asleep and left the game early, and the moment everyone remembers from that night was him picking a random winner over a set of two cards that I had strategically and logically placed for a perfect combination. Stupid pennywhistle solo ...

We became closer over the ensuing few months, despite our seven-year age difference. That never came into play, except with his mother worrying about him being out with someone older, at times. But we were both partnered at the time and laughed at the worrisome manner in which people treated our friendship.

Well, I guess we weren't really fooling anyone.

We both broke up with our respective partners in April of 2014. Mine involved being broken up with via email after a two-year relationship and a dishonest move from our house, and his involved ... realizing I was available, I imagine. I only partially claim a joke in that regard.

The first night that we ended up spending together involved Bailey's and a lot of repressed feelings coming forth. We ended up sleeping until four p.m. the next day, with both of us awkwardly trying to make sense of everything.

Being that I'd just had my heart broken (again, but that's a story for another time), I wasn't in any hurry to rush into things. He stuck with me regardless of my best attempt to pretend our feelings weren't as strong and mutual as they were, but the more time we spent together, the more I fell in love with his heart.

The age difference was never a factor. He was there for me regardless of my mood or what was going on, and the more he was, the more I wanted him there in the difficult moments.

That summer, before certain events transpired that delayed everything, he saw me as my true self for the first time. We had a weekly theme for our game nights at my place, and he'd picked a drag night. Subtle, I know. I saw this as the opportunity to officially come out to the entire group, and it's quite obvious in the picture we got together that he was smitten.

I'd built up a protective layer of callous until that point, but I realized when I was out as Marissa, not only was I completely vulnerable, but I felt *everything* that much stronger, including how I felt about him. I felt alive, motivated, and like I wanted to kick the closet door down and be out as his girlfriend (we called it a lesbian thing at the time because he wasn't out yet).

He came out to me about six months later, in the most

off-handed and awkward manner possible. Again during a game of Cards Against Humanity, he mentioned to the people we were playing with that he was trans, and my surprise at the moment wasn't that he was, but that was the way he chose to tell me.

Despite not being attracted to men, it took me about a day to adjust my thinking in regard because I'd fallen in love with his heart first, and that didn't change no matter what gender he was. If anything, we were more connected and open with each other than we ever had been. He started taking on some of the more "traditional" male roles, but our relationship as equals only changed in what we called each other, and the pet names that resulted from that sweetness that gives others the diabeetus.

He also proposed via text message after a long night at a con, so it was only fitting that everything that transpired in our relationship was surprising and awkward, especially since we both are anyway. I wrote about our wedding in *The PC Lie*, so I won't cover that again, but if anything has strengthened as much as my resolve for justice and equality, it's my love for him.

The pinnacle of this was at the 100th episode of *Inciting Incident*, which was held in the same place we got married about five weeks short of a year to the day that we got married. We'd gotten married under our deadnames because we weren't out to some of our family yet, but most of the people there knew. Nonetheless, a wrong needed to be righted.

After planning it with the theater rep, who was by no coincidence the same person who officiated our wedding, I had a shotgun wedding renewal in front of our closest friends and contemporaries, hitting everyone right in the feels in between Rissy being so nervous about the show that she drank while forgetting to eat. I think that was the most memorable part of the show for everyone.

The best part of the story is that I grew up calling Becky my sister, almost hyperbolically, in the way that close friends feel like siblings in their relationships. However, once I married her younger brother, suffice it to say that she became my legal sister-in-law, so there's a real sense of irony and foreshadowing retrospectively.

Sometimes life has a way of working out in ways you'd never expect, despite the evidence and planted seeds being right in front of you.

COMING OUT ADULT

AMINA SHEPHERD

I always knew I was different than other girls, even when I was growing up. I mean, when you spend as much time in your puberty years noticing the long legs and developing chests of your female friends as the pecs of your male running mates, you kinda sorta know you are not the typical, normal, all-American, apple pie-snorting straight girl.

I just didn't know what to call it. Bisexual was not something they discussed in Sunday school, or even sex ed, back then. I didn't know anyone gay except my cousin T, and the family saw him as a freak, so he was no role model. It took me years to finally look myself dead in the face and say, "You're an adult woman who likes men and women, and the world is not coming to an end."

In fact, it feels more normal than ever. Whatever normal is. I don't think normal really exists. Normal is different in each person's eyes.

But yeah, I'm bisexual, and that's okay. It's okay if family and exes tell me I'm going to hell. It's okay if friends don't understand or think I'm magically straight if I'm with a man (which I'm not). It's okay if my mom tells me she just wants me happy, but she doesn't completely get it. She doesn't completely get Google, either, and I still love her.

I'm bisexual, and also in love with a beautiful transwoman who loves me back. And that's okay. It's all okay. It's more than okay.

It's normal.

WHAT TO EXPECT WHEN YOU'RE
TRANSITIONING

MARISSA ALEXA MCCOOL

Being a visible and openly trans activist as I am, I get emails or messages a lot from people who might be starting to question their gender, or from loved ones of those who are questioning.

While I am certainly willing to take as much time as necessary to have those messages, Skype calls, etc., I feel like I should put out a list of some of the things I say in these conversations, especially because I know for everyone who reaches out, there are many more who are afraid to initiate the conversation, afraid that I won't have time to listen, or any other reason.

Therefore, I'm publishing this post for those who may not feel able to talk to me, publicly or privately, and may be in a position of having gender questions.

A note: These pieces of advice are based on my own experience, my experiences with other trans people, the numerous interviews conducted herein, and the books I've read authored by other trans people. This is by no means an end-all, be-all guide, and before you make any major decisions, you should talk to a trusted LGBT-friendly doctor so that you're well-aware of other baggage that may come with this decision. I'm not a professional (at medicine, anyway), and do not claim to be an expert, only someone with a lot of personal experience.

NO MATTER HOW OPEN-MINDED OR GENDER-BLIND YOU THINK YOU ARE, THERE ARE SOCIETAL INFLUENCES, TOXIC THOUGHTS, AND OTHER PRESSURES YOU NEED TO SORT OUT IN YOUR HEAD.

Our participation in this culture is not as manageable as your Facebook feed, meaning, you can't always filter out what you don't like or want. Culture, on a basic level, is learned behavior, and we don't always choose what we learn on a subconscious level. You may have harmful perceptions of gender, relations, and how one should act that may detract from your experience.

When you're first starting to question your gender, a lot of those things are going to come up, possibly as reasons why you shouldn't transition. They might look or sound like:

- I don't want to be called by male/female/neutral pronouns because no one will ever respect that, anyway.
- I don't want to admit to myself that I'm trans because I see how the community is treated in certain parts of society.
- I don't think I could ever go through with surgeries or HRT.
- I feel like there may not be a point in coming out or transitioning.

All of these are valid, and yet they're sometimes defense mechanisms we've created to talk ourselves out of taking that leap.

Make no mistake about it, these questions are difficult, deeply embedded in your consciousness, and may bring about thoughts and memories you wish they didn't. However, once you get past all the reasons you think it'll never work, once you can sort all those in another folder, that is when you can truly start asking yourself the most important questions.

- Why am I questioning my gender?
- What does gender mean to me?
- How do I really feel?
- Who do I really think I am?
- Does it truly matter what anyone else thinks of it?

Once you can get to those without talking yourself out of even thinking about it, then you can truly start to learn who you are.

YOUR ANSWERS MAY CHANGE.

Coming out/being trans isn't always as easy as "I always knew." As much as some stories would like to have you think that, exploring and discovering your gender identity is a deep, long, and difficult experience, and the answer may change.

I, for one, talked myself out of coming out numerous times, got scared and went back into the closet, then talked myself out of HRT, then talked myself out of surgery, and the list goes on.

If you don't feel like you can or want to go on hormones, you don't have to to be valid. If you don't feel like you could ever go through with surgery, fine! You don't have to go through any procedure to be valid in who you are. Don't let the outside world move the goalposts on you, because they will every chance they get.

Maybe you'll start in non-binary identities and move through them to the other side. Maybe you won't. Maybe you'll go with it for a while and then "de-transition." Maybe a non-binary identity is where your heart truly lies. And maybe that answer will change over time too!

It doesn't matter. This is your journey, and nobody can take that away from you. Nobody has more of a right to your identity than you do, despite what the anti-trans commentators would have you believe.

DON'T LET CONCERNS OVER BEING ABLE TO "PASS" TALK YOU OUT OF EMBRACING YOUR IDENTITY.

Remember what I said about moving the goalposts. Some people will tell you the only way you can be valid in your trans-identity is by "passing" according to cisgender standards. Those who can stealth or not be visibly trans, that's what some would like us to believe is the only valid way.

You don't owe anyone in this society, including yourself, blending in by cis standards. Your journey isn't about them or living up to how they feel you should be adequately trans. Despite what some insecure people may think, our lives are not devoted to blending in to trick people into accidentally being attracted to trans people.

GIVE YOURSELF TIME, DISTANCE, AND RECOVERY.

Being online and trans sucks sometimes.

By that, I mean if you're like me, not a day goes by where

someone in your Facebook feed, or one of their friends, doesn't have something shitty to say about trans people.

Even the proudest among us, it gets to us after a while. Allow yourself time away. Allow yourself space to recover. Take time away from those toxic arguments. You're not obligated to speak up if you don't want to, and you don't have to chime in on every douchebag who says an inappropriate thing. Trust me, that urge is there, and gets magnified if you get into activism.

Be proud, be as loud as you feel safe being, but don't feel like you have to rebut every terrible argument. None of us have the time for that.

Right now, I'm on a self-imposed Facebook ban until I get back home from a weekend getaway. I imposed this ban on myself because getting into too many arguments and/or constantly trying to validate or justify my humanity and right to my identity finally caught up with me.

And if you've listened to any of my shows, you know I yell a lot. Give yourself that time away; we all need time to recover, recharge, and distance ourselves from the toxic opinions of those who may never understand us.

YOU DON'T OWE CIS PEOPLE ANYTHING.

This is the main reason I've been on hiatus: defending this ideal. Whether it's people who think we owe them our trans status immediately, or those who feel entitled to have us answer their questions at any time, no matter how invasive they are, you don't owe anybody anything. Nobody is entitled to your time. Nobody is entitled to your body. Nobody has the right to demand something from you that you're not ready to give them.

YOU'RE NOT OBLIGATED TO FIT SOMEONE ELSE'S STANDARDS OF MASCULINITY, FEMININITY, ETC.

When my husband got deeper into his transition, he started wearing makeup and short shorts again. At a point, he was afraid to, because he felt he had to live up to some standard of masculinity that he'd felt influenced by.

Dispel yourself of that toxic bullshit as quickly as possible. You can be a trans woman and wear jeans and a t-shirt. You can be a trans man and wear makeup and like cute things. You can be non-binary and still associate with things you liked before you came out. Let yourself like things because you like them, not because you think you should.

YOU WILL HEAR EVERY STUPID ARGUMENT, NO MATTER HOW LONG YOU'RE OUT AND NO MATTER HOW MUCH YOU TRY TO AVOID THEM.

Here, I'll knock a few out right now ...

Not disclosing trans status is dishonest. Trans is a fad. Trans was made up by Tumblr in 2009. There are only two genders. You can't change gender.

Chromosomes. DNA. Science. You're still X no matter what. You're a distraction. You're sick. You need help.

Trans is a mental illness. Trans people have magic, gender-bending mind powers because they're sorcerers whose mission in life is to spread the trans and play volleyball in the face of mocking god.

Okay, maybe that last one is true. The rest are absolute bullshit mostly perpetuated by people who aren't trans, don't know anyone who is trans, don't know the first thing about being trans or HRT or anything else, or do have some of those things and still perpetuate harm to others.

Fuck them.

I say this often: I'm openly trans because I want to be, not because I feel obligated to be so in order to make others more comfortable. I was transitioning five months before I came out publicly.

This journey is about you. Figure out who you are, figure out what you want, and find your own identity. You don't have to accept what others tell you that you are. You don't have to accept the naysaying in the back of your mind that tells you you'll never be valid/accepted/passing/trans-enough/etc.

Make this journey because you want to. Make this discovery because you want to. Be who you are because you want to ... Not because others feel entitled to that information or your answers to their questions.

I regret nothing about who I am. I only wish I'd had access to the information I did much earlier in life. I would've transitioned over a decade ago if I'd known that was an option.

Be sure to talk to people you trust. Don't risk your life, house, job, or safety over it if you can help it. Read or listen to things that other trans people have said. Those who put it out there, myself included, partially do so in order to try to help make it easier on trans people coming out after we do.

Trans stories are as varied as trans people themselves, and I hope your story gives you the happy answers and experiences that my journey has for me. You deserve happiness, respect, and the freedom to be who you are, and don't ever let anyone, including yourself, convince you otherwise.

And, of course, reach out if you feel like you need to. I'm on Facebook at Marissa Alexa McCool, Twitter @RisMcCool, Instagram @littlegirlrissy, Snapchat @rissymonster, or you can email me at rismcwriting@gmail.com. I always try to answer as many and as quickly as possible, and there are plenty of other openly trans people who are willing to answer your questions when they can.

Don't be afraid to find out who you are because of what you're worried may happen. Find out. It's worth it. Even with all the pain, negative things, and societal attachments that come with being openly trans, I don't regret a thing. I just need time to take care of myself sometimes.

Don't we all?

STAGE FRIGHT
LOGAN REISS

The lights come on. I'm standing on my own section of a stage, yet I'm not the only one on stage. The lights are bright in my eyes as the people in the audience watch, judge, pay close attention to every movement and every sound that comes out of my mouth.

Improvisation. Uncertainty. Despair.

I am consumed by loneliness, fear.

I am on my own.

As a child, being different was always the hardest thing I had to face. I had to learn to improvise, learn how to act, learn to hide, lie, and start over. As the transition into adulthood slowly occurs, so does my transition into who I really am, who I want to be, and how I look at myself. Who I am is okay, and I will not act differently any longer.

Even to my own communities, I am different. I am not a girl, yet I wear makeup. I am not feminine, yet I enjoy jewelry. I am an artist, yet my canvas is sometimes biological. I am outside the binary, yet I find comfort in the label "transgender." I am not neurotypical, yet my neurodivergence does not define me. I am not a stereotype, so I am and always have been set aside as wrong.

So I acted. By day, masked normality, and by night, a shell. When I wanted to wear pants to church, my parents would tell me a dress was better. So I would wear a dress. When I wanted to cut my hair short, I listened to people who told me long hair was better. When I felt that being called a girl was wrong, I shut up.

When I identified with male fictional characters, I didn't tell anyone. When I was told to act like a lady, I did. When I was told makeup was for women, I wore makeup. When I was told that every girl has crushes on boys, I pretended to have crushes.

When I went out with my family, I did not say what I wanted and instead said what they wanted to hear. I was the perfect child, as long as I stayed ignorant.

It's humbling to look back and see how people saw me and how I saw myself. Others saw me as a goodie-two-shoes; I saw myself as someone who was not able to put myself in danger. Others saw me as girlish and outgoing; I saw myself as manly and introverted. Others saw me as smart; I saw myself just getting by until I could do what I loved.

Others saw me as normal; I saw myself as anything but.

My character was ruled by the directions of others. When I started being myself all the time, people I had loved turned against me; I had to find people I could really trust and rely on. My parents ignored what I was passionate about and who I was, my old friends thought I was disgusting, the person I thought I would spend eternity with left me because they suspected that I was lying or confused.

I found loss and gain and betrayal and friendship during that time in my life. The tragedy and comedy of my life played out to find the heroes and the villains throughout the cacophony of dissonant notes.

Looking back on my past is like looking at a recording of an improv act. No one knew how well it would go or where it would go, but now we're here and we have to make something of that.

Sometimes the cast changes or the setting moves, or the themes and genres blur, but it is still my story to make my own. Making jokes to fill the silence and learning to see the other people who are standing with me is important in getting over the fear of having the spotlight in my eyes. The world is my stage, and I don't have lines to memorize anymore.

MANY A MONOLOGUE

MARISSA ALEXA MCCOOL

A theater group at Penn was putting on the seventeenth production of *The Vagina Monologues*. The director of the show was my friend Pearl, with whom I'd taken Introduction to Acting in 2013 with Dr. Rosemary Malague.

In that class, we'd shared a scene that taught us the connection beyond the words of the script, and I think that really bonded us. She'd followed my transition from a distance, but reached out because she had an opening in the show for a small part. Naturally, I was more than willing to accept any chance to be on stage, so I was going to be part of the show.

The previous year, my friend Chris had asked me to be a part of her show, but at that point, I wasn't ready to be so open about my transition. It wouldn't be too long before she asked me again, and this time, I accepted that one as well. The latter one had given me the trans monologue for the show, but in the Penn one, it was already taken. I had my issues with that, but that's not what this story is about.

As the day approached, I'd found the perfect dress for the occasion; a mostly black swing dress with a red bow in the middle, thus fitting the standard dress code of the show. I'd gotten some high black boots to go with it, and they made me feel gorgeous. If there was one place I wasn't afraid of my height, it was on stage where you wanted to be as tall as possible anyway.

I'd been on stage hundreds of times, and even done a couple of standup performances as my true self, but this was theater. This was a place where I thrived. This was one of the few places where my passions truly lay. I didn't have a big part; I was only introducing another monologue, as the show was set up to include as many people as possible, so instead of the narrator introducing each piece, another performer would do so.

I was also included in a small bit part in the final monologue, the one about the sex worker who pleased other women. The director had a fun idea for the part where kinds of orgasms are impersonated, and I had the last one, notoriously titled the "State of the Union" orgasm, which satisfied my desire and ability to *ham* it up.

It was also going to be very special for me because some of my closest friends were coming. My LaLa, who readers might be more familiar with as Lucinda Lugeons from the *Scathing Atheist* podcast, would be traveling with me for it one night, along with my friend Kim. Another night, my friend Kelly, whom I affectionately referred to as my "Penn pal," would be in attendance with her boyfriend.

For the most part, though, I was an unknown to the audience and the cast. Being a commuter for four years hadn't provided me with many opportunities to get to know people outside of school, not to mention the age and class disparity for the most part at a university like that.

Pearl had me come there early so she could do my makeup, which she did a fantastic job of, by the way. One of the pictures I took on stage before the show remains one of my two favorite publicity photos, despite it being so much earlier in my transition. Even *Cognitive Dissonance* used it when they interviewed me much later.

The most important part of this story, though—at least the Penn part—took place before the show started. At that time, the entire cast gathered in a giant circle and anyone could say what was on their mind.

Haters might call it a "safe space" in a pejorative sense, but that's exactly what it was. Any lady could say anything she wanted about anything. No claps but snaps, nothing left the room, and everyone was joined together and supportive; it was the safest I'd felt in my entire life.

On top of that, though, it was a truly welcoming space. Nobody misgendered me. Nobody deadnamed me. Nobody questioned why I was there. That wasn't common in my first few months of transition. It gave me the courage to read something I'd written in hopes the director could get Eve Ensler to let me perform it.

By that, I mean that the show has a strict license about improvised or cast-created material, and it had to be approved if the show wanted to keep its license. They were unable to obtain it, but they compromised by printing part of it in the program for the show, which was nice of them.

But I had it there, in my hand, and the environment that cast room created made me feel safe enough to read it.

This piece is published in *Silent Dreams*, but I'll share it here anyway, in case you haven't read that book, or seen the videos or postings of this performance:

Once Unspoken
A Monologue

To the world, I'm 31. To myself, I'm 13.
13 years ago, that's when I got my name.

The name that would stick in my mind,
The name I would crave to be called,
The name that made me cry at night,
The name that made me wish it'd gone away,
That was the name that stayed in my heart.

A drag queen is what I thought I was,
Because I didn't know any better.
We weren't educated on such things.
Even the open-minded among us,
To our groups, conversations, and movies,
Transpeople existed only as
Jokes
Punch-Lines
Comedy
Fodder
Plot Twists.
That was all we knew.

Drag queen is what I let them call me,
To pretend that I was laughing with them,
Instead of believing the laughter was at me.
But I loved the makeup, the clothes, the shoes,
The way my eyes looked with mascara,
The way my legs felt smooth to the touch,
The way I felt unapologetically myself,
And nobody could take that from me.

But I had to keep it a secret.
It was too much for some people to handle.
They thought I should be a real man,
Be a provider, protector, breadwinner,
The cuddler, the kisser, the initiator,
Even those who said they understood,

Appreciated the dynamic,
Thought it was kinda hot,
Always defaulted to the traditional expectation.
Too emotional, too needy, too affectionate,
"Stop trying to be the little spoon!"
"Stop being scared at loud noises!"
"Stop wearing such bright colors!"
"Stop skipping, stop dancing, stop singing,
Stop wearing eyeliner, stop tilting your head,
Stop putting your hand on your hip,
Stop being so…
Girly!"

Growing up pretending to be a boy,
Girly was the worst thing you could be.
You play like a girl, you cry like a girl,
You were a pussy if you were weak,
You were a girlfriend if you didn't like guns,
Girls couldn't rape guys because,
Huh-huh, you can't rape the willing, LOL, right?
Hey baby, you don't need the gun!
High-five, bro!

I craved to be protected.
I adored feeling like people wanted
To stand up for me
To let me cry
To let them be there for me,
But I couldn't.
I wasn't being honest with myself
Because I was scared.
Terrified.
What would the world think?
What would my parents think?

What would happen to me?
Would I be bullied?
Beaten?
Assaulted?
Killed?

Then I found the Queer Dictionary.
I read through the words, the labels, the definitions.
I wasn't a drag queen.
I wasn't a crossdresser.
Transgender though, that seemed right.
But it was too much commitment.
So I went with gender queer,
Non-binary,
Genderfluid,
Gender nonconforming...
Anything that allowed me to be Marissa,
But not take the full jump.
No hormones, no shots, no meds,
Nothing permanent.
Permanent was scary.

However, as I became Marissa,
I stopped liking being called sir.
I began to hate my deadname.
I began to hate being associated as a guy,
A male,
A him,
A dude,
A bro,
Thank you very much, sir.
Have a nice day, sir.
Is this your husband?
Is this your father?

I wanted to be one of the girls.
I wanted to be a girl.
I... am a girl.
I couldn't even commit to it when I went on HRT,
But my spouse referred to me as Marissa,
Ris,
Rissy Monster,
Princess,
Baby.
He called me beautiful, precious,
Pretty, princess, baby girl...
All the things I wanted to be called my entire life,
But wasn't allowed.
Cause that'd be gay, right?

But then...
Then two people took from me.
Like thieves in the night, they stole.
They took my body.
They took my rights.
They took my voice.
They took
My consent.
I hid.
I ran.
I fled.
I became numb.
Distant.
Vacant.
I cut my hair.
Ditched outfits.
Tossed aside the makeup.
Died inside every time someone called me Alex,

But I dealt with it.
Because that's what the world was like
To people like me
If I was true.

Then one day, he came to our school.
Pastor Carl.
Filled with hate,
Bigotry,
Moral superiority,
Slurs,
Threats,
Damnation,
Scare-tactics,
Humiliation,
And self-righteousness.
He called girls sluts,
Gay people words I won't repeat,
And trans acceptance was the reason
Penn had a suicide problem.
Not because of bullies like him,
But because being who we are
Was subconscious defiance of truth.
That's why we hurt,
That's why we suffered,
That's why we died,
Because Pastor Carl knew the truth
And we ran from it.
We only chose to be who we were
To mock God.

As I stood up to him,
I was no longer afraid.
Nothing he said could touch me.

Nothing he said could penetrate my shield.
Nothing he said mattered.
So I yelled directly in his face:
"I'm transgender, fuck you!"
And that was it.
I was out.
I was Marissa.

Then we got a new President,
And all hell broke loose.
The same fear I'd had for years,
Seemed to consume the many.
So I wrote,
Yelled,
Podcasted,
Published,
Guested,
Stood up,
Stood out,
Owned who I was,
And within three months,
I was Marissa fuckin' McCool.
Published author,
LGBT columnist,
Trans-podcaster,
Guest on God Awful Movies,
And now, performing in the Vagina Monologues.
As me.
As Marissa.
As Marissa Alexa McCool.
Who I've always been.
True.

Tonight is not my first, or even hundredth

Time on stage in public,
But it is the first time,
The very first time,
That any cast list or program
Will read: Marissa Alexa McCool.
And that, my dear friends,
Was worth every step of the journey.

I read it much faster than I would in later performances, almost Noah Lugeons-diatribe style, and every single person in that room was attentive, supportive, and emotional.

Even though the safe time went on for another forty-five minutes, there were many hugs and words exchanged because of it, and I felt like I belonged. Those women brought me into their most intimate group space, allowed me to speak, and accepted me for who I was: one of them. No questions asked about what was in my pants or what my former name was, just... Welcome, Marissa.

Or, as some people would call it, the real problem with millennials and SJWs these days.

Walking out on stage that night, it was electric. The lines I delivered got laughs, the end of my part was cheered, and I sat on stage as the rest of the show was performed without question or anxiety.

The hardest part, however, was the end of the show, where everyone who has been sexually assaulted or worse stands up in unison. That's where the weight of everything I'd been through hit me. That's where I realized how important the work I needed to do truly was. That's where my priority shifted to women and LGBT people much more so than the skeptic and atheist community.

Later that year, the #MeToo campaign would have a similar effect on many more people.

The second night of the show went very similarly, with a much bigger crowd. I didn't read the monologue again to the cast, but I still thanked them for welcoming me into their space and making me feel accepted. I bonded with several of the cast members in a way that I'd only dreamed about and imagined before. Many of these women I would never see again, at least possibly until next year's show, but for that night, it was stronger than most connections I'd ever had in my life.

The main reason I know that was the second time I stood up at the end. Things hit me a lot harder that night. As the speech about sexual assault was given, I thought about everything that had happened to me in that regard.

I thought about being roofied in the bar. I thought about being taken against my will in my own room. I thought about my former bosses and co-workers, about the people who bullied me online, back in school... the ones who beat me with a baseball bat in my own driveway when I was just sixteen...

Everything came to my mind at once.

The tears started streaming down my face despite me trying to hide them, as I was in the front row on stage. I couldn't duck behind anyone or obscure the view in any way. When the moment came to stand, the two people beside me not only stood up with me, but held my arms in solidarity and comfort. I had the bittersweet moment of feeling simultaneously destroyed and rebuilt, and it changed my life forever.

The moment I got offstage, Pearl hugged me tighter than possibly any person who wasn't already married to me ever had. If Pearl Lo is not known to you at this point, I assure you that she will be someday. That lady has the empathy, intelligence, and motivation to become a person that everyone will have the chance to know for the work she does, and I'll one day be able to say that I was proud to know her when...

The story about the VagMons doesn't end there. After the show, an article was published about how this was the first time transgender cast members were ever a part of the show. I'm not sure if there were other trans people in the show, but I also didn't ask. It wasn't my place.

Being one of the first, if not *the* first trans person to be in that show in seventeen years on a campus that prided itself in involvement and inclusion, though... that was a bit worrisome.

Shortly after the show, I received an invite from a group on campus to read the piece I'd written at a night of quiet performance. It was at a (are they still called frat?) house, and I was interviewed by the school paper again about the monologue I'd performed, and also the follow-up piece where I reflected on the journey. That one, also published in *Silent Dreams*, is here:

Snapshot of Transcience

To be free
To live true
To let go of the burden of secret
Is to truly see the world.

The blade of a pine,
A snow-covered mountain,
The everbrightening shimmer
Of the morning sun
Over quickly melting snow;

I see the colors anew,
The nature therapy

Checks me in
As a returning guest.

All around me
The sentiment of serenity
The spectacle of unconquered,
I am rendered
As a mere humbled patron
Of its healing grace.

Departing is so sorrow,
Walking over again
The tracks created
To reach the momentary
Blissful seconds of clarity.

But a selected glimpse
Though it may be
Toward the mountains
Yet to climb
Along the seemingly infinite horizon,
My journey is no longer
Perpetually weighed down
By the heaviest of unseen burdens:
The burdening secret
Of identity.

I am far more
Than a sum
Of the parts I didn't choose.

I am the Planet of one,
The waking oblivion of bliss,
The anxious headspace

Of the purple girl Ris.

Though a long way
To go remains,
I travel lighter
Having shed the baggage
With the mask of my former shield.

I walk the more dangerous path
By choice of not to hide,
But they who've embraced me
Shelter me from
Any pangs of regret
For which I may search
Among the discarded.

This is true,
This is right,
This is me,
The me that you knew,
But the mirror did not
Until I gazed
At the correct reflection.

Previously untouched,
Formerly shamed,
Now a cloud of the spirit
Of mystic joy;
I am now but a protected
Nomad of these parts,
And I'm for long so grateful
Of permission of minute occupation
Along the intersecting trails
Of your own journeys

Yet untraveled.

But of course, that's not the end of this story.

Remember how I mentioned my friend Chris—the person who ministered my wedding, by the way—had also invited me to be a part of her show? I had that to look forward to as well, and that would be a completely different environment. It was held at The Carlisle YWCA, a town where I'd lived, and people I knew were going to be there. More than I'd thought at the time, but I'm getting ahead of myself.

In this show, the monologues weren't memorized, they were read. That took a lot of pressure off the performers and instead allowed the moments to be captured with as pure of emotion as possible.

Where the Penn cast had seventy performers, this one had about seventeen, and this time I'd found a formal gown and made the mistake of also trying to wear stiletto heels. Those didn't last the whole show, surprise, surprise.

In the cast room before the show, I wanted to recreate at least a semblance of the moment I'd had with the Penn cast of ladies, so I asked if I could read the monologue I'd written. I performed it much the same way I had in the Penn cast room.

One thing was different about this one, however. The moment I finished, Chris looked at me and said, "Screw the license, you're reading that one."

Holy shit, I needed to edit!

I brushed up the monologue a bit, even updating some of the words and adding a few things that had changed since I'd written it the first time. I knew there would be some improvisation as well, and that would be okay too. Nobody knew it but me, so if I changed a word or added a line, no one would be the wiser.

Despite being introduced under the wrong name, I gave a much different performance of the monologue this time. Line by line, I took every moment I could to let each piece of the monologue hang in the air, full of emotion and raw vulnerability. I owned it, and put my heart on the line in a way that I never truly had before.

At the end, when I delivered the line about making all the difference, the entire cast rose. The entire audience rose. I was given a standing ovation for my piece, and it lasted for what seemed like several minutes, but was likely only ten seconds or so.

Regardless, it was the greatest personal moment of my life. It gave me a feeling of validation, empathy, compassion, and continued to light the fire that had been burning inside me ever since I wrote "fuck you" in *The PC Lie* and continued from there. I was electric.

This story has an epilogue too.

In addition to my family who were waiting for me, one person stood behind me with her arms crossed and a knowing gaze. I turned as Aiden pointed her out, and a very long story arc reached its conclusion at that very moment in time.

It was Susan; the girl who put makeup on me in high school, one of the people who when I came out had said she'd known all along... *That* Susan. The hug she gave me encapsulated nearly fifteen years of confusion, worrying, depression, anxiety, internalized transmisogyny, and the loss of hope as well as its regaining.

At that moment, I truly was Marissa-fucking-McCool. Who I always had been. Who I always would be. Who I'd always wanted to be, doing as I'd always wanted to do: being on stage, being honest, and owning the moment in a way that I could.

I was valid. I was beautiful. I was a girl.

I was, entirely, Marissa.

ABOUT THE AUTHOR

Marissa, 32, is a wife, partner, parent, podcaster, activist, speaker, and now an author of five books. She graduated the University of Pennsylvania cum laude in 2017 with degrees in English, Cinema and Media Studies, and Anthropology. She has been published by *The Huffington Post, Psychology Today, Lords of Pain, Intentional Insights, Faithless Feminist, Snarky Feminist,* and her own blog, *Marissa Explains it All,* not to mention countless guest spots on podcasts in addition to her own shows.

For more information:
rismccool.com
rismcwriting@gmail.com